QUEER
HOLINESS

QUEER
HOLINESS

The Gift of LGBTQI People to the Church

CHARLIE BELL

DARTON·LONGMAN + TODD

To Graeme, Kathryn and Piotr – love is eternal

First published in 2022 by
Darton, Longman and Todd Ltd
1 Spencer Court
140 – 142 Wandsworth High Street
London SW18 4JJ

ISBN: 978-1-913657-92-5

A catalogue record for this book is available from the British Library.

Printed and bound in Great Britain by Bell & Bain, Glasgow

CONTENTS

ACKNOWLEDGEMENTS

This has been a book a long time in gestation, but in the end was one that really wrote itself. This topic has never been far from my mind and I have been lucky to have met so many people – Christian and otherwise – who have encouraged and supported me on the way. I am particularly grateful to the churches in which I have lived, worshipped and served, who have enabled me to be myself in way that doesn't require me to constantly justify who I am.

There are, of course, far too many people to thank to name here. However, there are some people I would particularly like to thank. It goes without saying that none of this is directly their fault, and any errors are my own. Nonetheless, none of this would have happened without them.

Firstly, Fr Mark Williams, Fr Nick Quanrud, and the entire clergy and people of St John the Divine, Kennington. It is a truly life-giving church, and one that I am deeply proud to serve – a beacon of hope and a place of great faith and love. Thanks too to Dean Andrew, Canon Michael and the whole team and congregation at Southwark Cathedral, who made me so welcome during my training for ministry, and Fr Paul and the people of St Paul's Deptford for their steadfast support and encouragement to smash oppression! These places - like so many in Southwark and beyond – model what it is to strive to be a truly inclusive community of faith, and a place where being LGBTQI is not only tolerated but embraced and welcomed. I would particularly like to thank Jessica Kingsley, from the Southwark Cathedral congregation, who was wonderfully encouraging and supportive when I went to her with the bonkers idea of writing a book, and who has prodded me in the right direction all the way.

I am grateful too to such a wonderful group of friends who have sustained and supported me over the years in my – at times, surely quite annoying – quest for justice. Particular thanks to Dr Emma Syea, Fr Tomos Reed, Fr Calum Zuckert, Dr Harrison Carter, Chris Douse, my former co-churchwarden Judith and her husband Richard Tonry, Drs Amita and Dirk Schuth, the wonderful St Augustine's gang (the inestimable and glorious Jules, and deacons Lizzie, Janice, Donna, Tim, Ben, Anthea, Rupert and Helga), Mthr Helen Harknett, Deacon Diane Kutar, Fr Mark Payne, Fr Steve Hilton, Fr Matthew Crane, Fr Jamie and Carol Hawkey, Canon Leanne Roberts, and Canon Anna Matthews – the latter two of whom are almost entirely to blame for my having been made deacon! Thanks too to Fr Ian Chandler, Fr David Lawrence-March, Fr Rob Mackley, Fr Malcolm Guite, Dean Nicholas Frayling, Canon Tim Schofield, Fr Alan Gregory and St Augustine's College, Mthr Clare Herbert, Fr Lyndon van der Pump, Fr John, Canon Simon Godfrey, Canon James Mustard, Fr Andrew Allen and all the extraordinary clergy who have supported and sustained me over the years, whatever their theological perspective – and particular thanks to Fr Tim Harling, the Dean of Queens' College, Cambridge, without whom none of this would have ever happened. Tim and Liz were wonderful friends to me during my time in Cambridge (and remain so!) and there is absolutely no question that I would have gone forward for ordination without their support.

There are a number of bishops I would like to thank, although I'm not sure it will do their careers much good! I would particularly like to thank Bishop Lindsay Urwin for getting me interested in the God thing in the first place, my diocesan Bishop Christopher Chessun for his gentle and kindly guidance, forbearance and wisdom, Bishop Peter Selby and Jan for their prophetic voices and generous welcome, and Bishop Stephen Conway for his encouragement to me to speak out when I was a seminarian (and before) in his diocese. Thank you, too, to Bishop David Hamid, who preached the first sermon I have ever personally heard from a bishop that clearly, explicitly and unequivocally recognised the equal human dignity of LGBTQI people, and to the late Bishop Morris Maddocks, who looked after me, together with Peter and Jane Kellett, during my years in Chichester. Bishop – pray for me! There are others, but I will not embarrass them here!

Thanks also to those who have spent decades challenging the Church of England to more fully live its vocation – those who have been unjustly treated, those who have suffered in public, those who have suffered in secret, and our even increasingly group of allies. There are too many to name here – but I salute you. Thank you to the campaigns that continue to push for change – Inclusive Church, Mosaic, the Jayne Ozanne Foundation, and the Campaign for Equal Marriage in the Church of England, to name a few. Jayne Ozanne took a chance on me to write for her brilliant *Via Media* blog, and without that chance, this book would never have happened. Too many people have had their ministry degraded or ended by the Church of England and it is only because of their courage - and the courage of those who support them – that change might indeed be possible. Too many, too, have left the Church, and even taken their own lives because of the oppression meted out to them by churches – this book is my own small contribution to honouring their memory.

Thanks too to the people of the various workplaces that I have found myself in over the past few years. I remain particularly grateful to Huw Yardley, my former boss at the Health and Social Care Committee of the House of Commons, for his careful and insightful chats and guidance, and to all the brilliant staff of South London and Maudsley NHS Foundation Trust. I have had the privilege of being a Fellow at two fantastic Cambridge colleges, Murray Edwards and Girton College, and I am immensely grateful to them for taking me on and being such vibrant, open and exciting places to be. I continue to pinch myself when I realise who I am sitting at table with when I am in college. If you are looking for an educational establishment that really gets the need for inclusion, and which – rather than sitting on its laurels – continues to strive to make things better, you need look no further than Girton. My students, the Fellows, the staff and the whole college community continue to inspire me and it has been a real honour to work in such a place. My particular thanks go to Professor Susan Smith, the Mistress, whose term of office is coming to a close, and who is a remarkable force for good, helping to make Girton the place that it is, to the marvellous Vice Mistress Emerita Karen Lee, my superb fellow Praelector Simone Maghenzani, and to my brilliant medical colleague Dr Fiona Cooke, who keeps me on the straight and narrow and has welcomed me to the college with such kindness. There are far too many Fellows to thank by name – to all of you, thank you.

David Moloney and the team at Darton, Longman and Todd, have been absolutely fantastic – easy to work with, encouraging and thorough. This is my first book, so I had no idea what to expect, but this is quite some standard to live up to!

My family have, I'm quite sure, given up trying to remember what I'm up to at any particular moment, and yet remain a wonderful source of support, fun and provide a much needed reality-check. Losing my father a decade ago was an absolute devastation for us all, but together we have continued to grow into an eclectic mix of people who remain – at heart – best of friends. Without the support of Kathryn, Graeme, Florence, Olivia and Harriet, and my bonkers yet brilliant grandparents Jean, John (by intercession in the heavenly realm), Effie and Angus (now also in glory), and my late father's brother John, I quite simply wouldn't be where I am today. Thank you to you all from the bottom of my heart – I certainly don't say it enough, so at least you now have it in writing. Thanks also to Fiona Mackay, my godmother, who has been the most brilliant and generous friend to my mother, and whose love and support over so many years I have valued greatly.

ACKNOWLEDGEMENTS

And last, but by no means least, Piotr. You are my strength and my stay – you put up with my grumpiness, my endless new 'good ideas', my constant need to use the study, my neurotic cleaning regime – the list is endless. I dare anyone to look in on our adventures and tell me that God disapproves. You are my everything and I adore you. Kocham Cię, babbington.

PREFACE

Is being gay a sin? For generations, this thorny issue has divided the Church, and whilst society has – at least in part – begun to recognise not only the importance of inclusion, but also celebration of the gifts of LGBTQI people, the Church lags miles behind. Of course, most church folk – even the most 'conservative' – would now say that being gay is not sinful in and of itself, but many nonetheless reject same-sex marriage as a worldly redefinition of a Christian institution, and in so doing, demand celibacy for swathes of LGBTQI people. Sexuality, outside these religious confines, is still deemed dangerous, and anyone who disagrees with this position 'simply doesn't know their Bible'.

This book has a simple premise – that however much we might know our Bible, if we exclude human experience, science and reason from the way we read and interpret that Bible, we not only do a poor job of interpretation, but in so doing, fail to take the Bible seriously or on its own terms. If we fail to meet God in the world as well as in the pages of scripture, then we end up with 'false limits of our own', as the great hymn goes.[1] The life of God revealed in scripture is one of narrative and of being alongside humanity – one in which the Son of God Himself became flesh and dwelt among us, and yet still we rejected Him. We don't appear to have learnt.

Its key contention is that the love between two people who want to commit themselves to each other is of the same

[1] 'There's a Wideness in God's Mercy', written in 1854 by the Roman Catholic convert Frederick Faber.

character, whatever sex or gender they might be. That love is expressed in relationship, which in many – indeed most – cases contains a sexual element, which is not something discrete but something integral to that relationship. Our denial of this relational sexuality to LGBTQI people is nothing short of scandalous. It is far more reflective of our cultural norms than a serious interrogation of the Bible in the light of lived reality.

Throughout Christian history, LGBTQI people have been scapegoated, and have been used as pawns in the wider game of church politics. They have been seen as acceptable collateral in international relations and consistently been targeted by religious authorities. They have been seen as dangerous and depicted as reckless and immoral. Their lives have been made targets of hilarity or abuse, and they have been reduced to an 'issue'. They have been blamed for dividing the Church and been told they hate the Lord, the scriptures, and the Church. They have looked for allies, asking 'who will go for us?', and too often met deafening silence. And yet they keep on worshipping the Lord.

This book has quite deliberately made use of the word 'LGBTQI' where possible – of course, some points will relate more to some members of the community than others, yet the underlying dynamic affects the whole. LGBTQI is not an exhaustive term – far from it – but it refers to those sexualities, sexual and gender identities that are so often pushed to the margins of the Church. It is those identities this book seeks to celebrate – not the notion of 'same-sex attracted' people that is so often heard in church circles. Same-sex attraction is not the defining feature of homosexual people, let alone all LGBTQI people, yet it is often the moniker that LGBTQI people are given. Being LGBTQI is about so much more than that – and being an LGBTQI Christian means finding our identity in Christ and yet not rejecting the human person that God has called us to be. These two are not in conflict – they are in synergy. LGBTQI identity is part and parcel of the Christian identity. Calling us 'same-sex attracted' cheapens this, and ties us to the bedroom – it suggests this is the core of who we are. All of us – straight or not – are 'same-sex attracted' in some way or form. A focus on this term in describing LGBTQI people points towards an unhealthy and quite unbiblical understanding of the human person.

This book is also quite consciously Anglican, set within the context of the Church of England. Specific examples are taken from this context, and its heritage is made use of in theological exploration. However, these issues – and more importantly, LGBTQI Christians – are, quite clearly, not only found in the Church of England. This book springs from the Anglican fountain, but the way of doing theology it recommends, and the way of engaging with LGBTQI people, is far more widely relevant. The more we remain siloed, the more challenging it is to bring in the Kingdom of Heaven.

There are relatively few footnotes found within this book, quite deliberately – it is not intended to be an exhaustive study of all the topics that it raises, but instead is an attempt to break apart lazy thinking, persuade readers of the validity of the questions it raises, and argue for an integrated and ultimately deeply theological way of seeking the face of God. It raises topics and studies in human discovery but does not seek to definitively pronounce on them. Most specifically, it does not pick and choose the studies that 'fit' (in the mode of some theological texts) but rather points the reader to areas of further exploration,[2] and to serious reviews of the scientific literature that are not compromised by theological bias. There is not space within these pages to do justice to the huge breadth of disciplines represented, but readers are encouraged to use this text as a stepping-stone that aims to

[2] Of particular interest to readers should be Thatcher, A. (ed.), *The Oxford Handbook of Theology, Sexuality, and Gender* (Oxford: Oxford University Press, 2015), which fleshes out many of the key points made here and offers ample suggestions for further reading. In addition, the following three books may be helpful companions: Ford, M., *God, Gender, Sex and Marriage* (London: Jessica Kingsley, 2018), Keen, K., *Scripture, Ethics, and the Possibility of Same-Sex Relationships* (Grand Rapids: Eerdmans, 2018), and Greenough, C., *Queer Theologies: The Basics* (London: Routledge, 2019).

justify the underlying method of doing theology.

Ultimately, however, this is a personal book. These 'issues' are personal to me, and personal to the huge number of people who are both LGBTQI and Christian. The life of LGBTQI Christians is fundamentally part of the life of the Church, not separate to it. We are – however much others might argue against our inclusion – equal citizens of the Kingdom of God, and we are not excluded by Christ from His Church. I love the Church, despite her failings, not because of some slavish devotion to an institution, but because she was founded by Christ Himself. When I look at the Church, I often ask – is this really the Church that God envisaged? I strongly believe that the Church needs not only to recognise LGBTQI people as beloved children of God, made in his image, and made for relational sexuality, but also take responsibility for the damage that it has done. The Church has failed to provide good role models for LGBTQI people and is far too often the cause rather than the opponent of prejudice. Many in the Church refuse to even recognise us as Christian.

This book is a call to action – for LGBTQI people, their allies, and the whole people of God. We are wounding the body of Christ if we do not repent and change the way we respond to LGBTQI people. It offers a vision of what is, and what could be. The choice is ours – corporately, and individually. There is no time like the present.

PART I

1

INTRODUCTION: WHERE ARE WE NOW?

The history of the Church and LGBTQI people is not a happy one.

LGBTQI people in the Church have spent a long time being told what God expects of them and how they should behave. From prohibitions on who they might love or marry, to erasure and denial, the theological record is one in which LGBTQI people are often objectified and their lives seen as the property of others. In recent decades, the Church has lagged behind wider society, and whilst even some conservative political movements have begun to recognise and fight for the rights of LGBTQI people, many in the Church have stubbornly refused to do so. LGBTQI people often remain 'a problem' – not as individuals, with their own lives, loves, hopes, dreams, disappointments and all the other mess of life, but as an abstract problem to be solved. Far too often, real lives are sacrificed on the altar of principle and seemingly immovable doctrine.

Doctrine, of course, is not the enemy of LGBTQI people. Christian doctrine, at its purest and most beautiful, is a set of beliefs and practices that fundamentally situate individuals and communities in a way that orients them most towards God. Christian doctrine is formed first and foremost by the grappling of the Church with the scriptures, and most particularly with the most holy of books, the Bible.

Christian doctrine looks towards the Word made flesh, Jesus Christ, and in the proclamation of his life, death and resurrection seeks to discern the will of God for humankind. Its basic premise is simple – that we most perfectly see the face of God and a human life fully lived when we look to the life of a Jew, born two millennia ago, who we recognise and acclaim as fully God and fully man. It is to God that we look for our very best anthropology: God, made man, living amongst us and dying for our salvation. This is the heart of the Christian faith, and this is the heart of Christian doctrine.

This book does not claim that doctrine *per se* is flawed, or that the Bible is anything but the record of God's revelation throughout history, culminating in the death and resurrection of the son of God on Calvary. What it seeks to do, however, is to take a step back from the perennial arguments around what the Bible does and doesn't say and resituate and re-evaluate the entire enterprise of doctrinal conversation by engaging with the world that God has given us. Doctrine is never about something abstract – it is about real lives, lived in a world that may be contingent but nonetheless was both created by and played host to the creator of the universe. Christian doctrine is not a set of Gnostic secrets or a set of abstract prescriptions for living – it is about the real, about the here and now. It is about flesh and blood, about a world saved through Christ and yet a world that remains beset by sin and death. It is about how we conduct ourselves when we go to the supermarket or down the pub. It is not simply about some part of us reserved for church on Sundays – it is an overwhelming, all embracing, total reorientation of our whole lives to God. It is ultimately that which speaks of human flourishing.

HUMAN FLOURISHING

Human flourishing is something that has excited and inflamed passions in human communities since the dawn of time. Every age and epoch, each ideology and theology, has its own particular view of what it is to be 'fully alive', to somewhat misquote St Irenaeus (to whom we will return later in this book). In recent centuries, we have heard arguments that show preference for community, and those that show preference for the individual. We have seen the rise and fall of communism, the continuing rise of capitalism and secular democracy in the west, and in recent times the reinvigoration of forms of religious politics in the middle east and beyond. Each ideology is based, at least in part, on a particular view of what human flourishing looks like – at a societal and at an individual level. The Christian faith likewise holds up its own version of human flourishing – that which points to the life of Christ in God. It is not merely ink that has been spilt in arguments around flourishing – far too much blood has been spilt, and continues to be, in the name of 'the greater good'.

The Christian narrative on human flourishing, of course, has not been linear, despite what certain parts of the Church might want us to believe. As an example, as more and more countries have opened up marriage to people of the same sex, a regular refrain has been that the state is trying to 'redefine marriage', and this must be opposed by all good Christians. That there has been one single understanding of marriage throughout Christian history is quite clearly nonsense;[1] and marriage is just the tip of the iceberg. All those things that contribute to human flourishing, or otherwise, and particularly feature in a Christian understanding – family, sex, love, life, war,

---

[1] Interested readers may wish to explore the works of Diarmaid MacCulloch, who has written extensively in this area. A useful starting point might be MacCulloch, D., *A History of Christianity: The First Three Thousand Years* (Oxford: OUP, 2010) and Thatcher, A., *The Oxford Handbook of Theology, Sexuality, and Gender* (Oxford: Oxford University Press, 2014).

punishment, power, justice, peace, and many more – have never had a static role in wider Christian belief.

Each generation of Christian believers, of many different strands of theological belief and practice, has refined, rethought and reimagined what in previous generations might have seemed entirely immutable. That is not the same as a blanket suggestion that what might be described as 'progress' in each generation is inevitably good, or that there are not core, central elements of Christian doctrine that remain unchanged and unchangeable. Yet it is unthinkable that some changes of the past would ever be seen as anything other than good – as being, indeed, of God. The abolition of slavery, the emancipation of women, even the decriminalisation of homosexuality – each of these is recognised, by most religious and secular authorities alike, as genuine progress in human understanding. The Holy Spirit may not be behind all secular 'progress', but to deny the Spirit's ability to act in the world and church, often in quite radical ways, is an equally absurd position to take. The challenge, of course, is identifying where the Spirit is acting – and finding criteria that are not simply subjective projections of one's inner prejudices and opinions.

It is easy for those who believe in the Gospel and in the role of the Church as God's agent in the world to become rather defensive about change that occurs outside the Church. Far too much time is given in contemporary church discussions to apocalyptic pronouncements about the world descending into chaos and the Church being threatened by the secular tyrannies that surround it. Hyperbole may sell newspapers and stir up crowds, but when such sweeping statements are made in the context of the life of the Church, hyperbole is only a paper-thin distance away from crass hypocrisy. It is staggering that such a view – that the world is inevitably bad and the Church inevitably good – continues to dominate so much of Christian thought. We need only look to the appalling abuse scandals, to the continued opposition to human rights – things that are demonstrably damaging to human flourishing – to see that the Church has nothing like an unblemished record. It is this demonstrable damage – and just as importantly demonstrable benefit from the ways of the world – that this book seeks to investigate.

Recognising that the Spirit works outside the institutional Church as well as within it may well prove challenging, particularly to those of a more 'conservative' bent. Yet it is important to state here what we are saying, and what we are not. Firstly, by recognising that the Spirit may work in the world, we are not calling everything the world does 'good', and nor are we saying that everything the secular world calls 'progress' is anything of the sort. This is not a wholesale rejection of the Church as that instituted by Christ – rather, it is a recognition that whilst the Holy Spirit may have been particularly gifted to the Church at Pentecost, the Spirit is nonetheless entirely able to work whither they choose. This is where the challenge comes in: when what the Church teaches comes into conflict with something in the world, and we are asked to discern where the Spirit is.

Of course, it is not down to us to choose – or at least, whatever we choose doesn't make it so. But there is something fundamental about 'discernment' at the heart of Christian theology, and about watching on the Holy Spirit to try to understand what God is doing in our context. This is nothing new – the Bible itself, as we shall discuss in Chapter 2, is a narrative that seeks to show and learn what God is doing in each age of His chosen people. Yet far too often, when it comes to questions of sexuality or gender, the natural response of 'conservatives' in the Church is to say that it is a rebellious world acting against the clear word of God in the Bible or in church teaching. Moves in human understanding of sex, sexuality and even human flourishing more widely are suspect, as if they are almost too dangerous to the Christian faith as to be allowed a full hearing. Yet this is the way that leads to ruin.

Such attitudes often lead to what is a false dichotomy

between the world and the Church – in which the Church is good, and the world is evil. Much is made of the Church's 'counter-cultural' position on sexuality, yet this is a simplistic reading that does not take history, nor even the present reality, seriously. It is certainly true that the Church of England's current position on sexuality is seen as, at very best, out of touch – and at worst, as morally bankrupt and evil – by a huge number of non-religious people. Yet far too often church people immediately jump from this to a self-righteous interpretation of John 15 (18-20; NRSV):

> 'If the world hates you, be aware that it hated me before it hated you. If you belonged to the world, the world would love you as its own. Because you do not belong to the world, but I have chosen you out of the world – therefore the world hates you. Remember the word that I said to you, "Servants are not greater than their master." If they persecuted me, they will persecute you; if they kept my word, they will keep yours also.'

Feigning persecution where there is none has, unfortunately, become one of the defining features of the contemporary church in western society – and is doubly offensive because of the genuine persecution some parts of the Church continue to face in other parts of the world. Nowhere has this been more evident than over questions of sexuality, where 'conservatives' frequently speak about how they are being persecuted for not following basic equalities legislation or because secular society doesn't support their right and desire to discriminate.

CHRISTIAN 'ORTHODOXY' AND THE CHRISTIAN COMMUNITY

Yet the Church has not always seen its opposition to LGBTQI rights as one of its measures of orthodoxy. Indeed, in a quite counter-cultural way, churches – including the Church of England in the 1960s – have on occasion opposed the discrimination shown by wider society to LGBTQI people, and instead argued for greater tolerance and acceptance. It is somewhat strange that homosexuality has become such a totem for orthodoxy, a key sign which many in the Church see as placing clear water between the 'good' church and the 'bad' world. The tired and overused phrase 'Bible believing' has become almost synonymous with anti-LGBTQI sentiment; churches that believe in the Bible cannot possibly support the rights of LGBTQI people, let alone encourage them to live fulfilled lives that encompass the whole of their person, sexuality included. A subculture of self-righteous discrimination has developed – we need only observe that being anti-gay is one of the key ways to get on in the GAFCON world, a group of churches that have broken away from full communion with the Anglican Church principally and primarily because of their fear that the Anglican Church has become too liberal on the 'gay issue'.

Churches in that orbit seemingly dare not even use the word 'gay' – instead, they refer to 'same-sex attraction', a pseudo-clinical term that sounds like something for which you need treatment. Yet, of course, these are the very same churches that do believe that treatment can be offered, and despite recent moves to ban conversion therapy, the most vociferous opposition comes from churches that see falling in love with someone of the same sex and wanting to express that with one's whole being as being a terrible affliction that must at least be avoided, if not cured. It remains somewhat confusing that the creeds can so lightly be set aside as the markers of orthodoxy, whilst a church's position on embodied expressions of love between two people of the same sex – something about which Jesus says absolutely nothing in the Gospels – is taken as the measure of a church's devotion to Christ. In a surprising move, it appears that 'conservative' churches care more about gay sex than a great many gay people.

The moniker 'same-sex attraction' in itself raises some significant questions, and amongst these is where the focus is during conversations on LGBTQI people. For those who cannot bring themselves to use the word gay, 'same-sex attraction' is a helpful phrase because it ultimately instrumentalises, and turns the 'acts' of homosexuality into the key feature, rather than, more properly, seeing them as an embodied manifestation or outward flowing of relational interconnectivity that is at the heart of healthy human flourishing. A focus on the external features makes it far easier to separate out the body and soul – a heresy so often happened upon when the whole human person is ignored at the expense of 'thou shalt nots', as we shall see in Chapter 2. 'Gay' is then described as a lifestyle, and that lifestyle as a choice – even if most churches are, at last, recognising that being attracted to people of the same sex is not something chosen but something given, and even gifted. The 'gay lifestyle' – a somewhat generic term that can be said to include whatever particular worldly 'outrage' some church folk might wish to include on any particular day – can then be condemned, as something against God and against His church. There again we meet good versus evil, church versus world – without a recognition that whilst such a simple delineation may make the life of the preacher easier, it doesn't necessarily reflect reality, and nor does it do justice to the action of the Spirit in the world.

It is interesting that many of the churches that appear to be most attracted to such a facile perspective are those which in other ways would definitively reject a spiritual notion of the Church and its traditions that might give it, as a corporate body, any particular role in salvation. Many of the most vehemently anti-LGBTQI churches speak at length of their reliance on scripture alone, and see no need to hold on to the traditional liturgy or historical practices of the Church. Yet in a sense, their identity as the Church is no less strong – albeit it is defined in a very particular, and defensive, way. For more catholic Christians, belonging to the Church is about belonging to something through the ages, that is more than human community and that is ultimately a vehicle through which God continues to act through the Spirit. For those who reject such a view, it is perhaps attractive, and social science would argue necessary, to form communities that have rules and beliefs as their defining and distinctive feature. This, perhaps, gives an insight into why a position on homosexuality has become such an important feature – it is something that can be directly measured against, it can be used in direct contrast to the 'values of the world', and it thus creates a sense of coherent community. Reliance on such a totem, however, is a position riddled with danger.

This is, then, an inherent risk with any theology that intentionally takes the metaphysical out of any understanding of the Church. If the Church is primarily a human community, rather than a participation in the communion of saints, then it becomes much more necessary to have a clear and specific set of rules against which to judge whether an individual is 'in' or 'out'. This leaves far less room for shades of grey, and creates an environment that is totally inhospitable to doubt or a lack of definitive clarity. As we shall see in Chapter 2, an attempt must then be made to turn the Bible into something that it is not, with all the consequences that that brings. In an interesting turn of events, it is only then a short distance to turning away from the 'justification by faith' of the Reformers to 'justification by works'. If belonging to a community requires a particular position on homosexuality, this is indeed primarily a matter of faith for those who are not LGBTQI – but for LGBTQI people, the picture becomes much more murky. Too often, it is these LGBTQI people within such communities of faith that are most easily forgotten, and most easily hurt. To be 'true Christians' in such a community requires them to act in particular ways without any focus on the underlying questions of human flourishing. It is here that the whole enterprise falls apart.

Any focus on the Church *as it is now* as the sole means of grace is one that is bound to fail. It is very easy to point fingers at wider society and bemoan the loss of a Christian society, but this fundamentally misunderstands how widely and deeply Christian values have infused into the world. In countries that have primarily professed the Christian faith for the past millennium, it is extremely difficult to extricate those things that are specifically 'Christian'. Indeed, one of the key problems is to identify what is genuinely Christian in what the Church has professed, taught and practised, and what is rather simply 'of the Church' and yet not of the Gospel. Yet it is certainly true that the Christian faith has fundamentally shaped much of our society, and shaped it in such a way that has seen continuous iteration and an inextricable link to Christian values throughout many of our institutions and in our public life, however uncomfortably this may sit with secularists. It is, then, absurd for us to cast such a dividing line between the Church and wider society, as though once the power and control over these values is ceded to wider society, they stop being Christian.

CHRISTIANITY AND WIDER SOCIETY

It is an entirely reasonable position to argue that LGBTQI rights have proceeded the way they have because of the Christian values that have been imbued into society. In a sense, society has been gifted these values and has run with them in ways which might never have occurred to the Church – two separate yet linked streams of thought that have run alongside each other and complemented each other in the process. Once again, not everything that happens in society, initially influenced by Christian values or otherwise, is good; but we simply cannot deny that God might be working through a society built on Christian foundations in a way that might surprise the Church – not least, surprise it because the conclusions it reaches may be different, and may challenge and act as corrective to the conclusions that the Church has itself reached. That so many in the Church are so scared of being corrected by society simply shows how far the Church has retreated into a defensive position, rather than being a place of dialogue and mutual respect.

We have seen a not dissimilar disaster in churches that have rejected possibly the greatest scientific development of the past millennium: the discovery of evolutionary processes. Faced with scientific developments like this, the Church has several options – it can embrace, it can critically analyse and be open to dialogue, or it can reject outright, making any such rejection a fundamental aspect of the Christian faith. This last option is, and has proved, catastrophic – it is a total rejection of human knowledge and leads to a church policy that will sink even the greatest apologist navy. Churches that currently make rejection of evolution a cornerstone of their faith – like several branches of American evangelical Protestantism that profess a six thousand year old Earth and make this a central tenet of their believing – are doomed to fail. There are only a few arguments that can possibly be made in this kind of situation – either that the scientists are wrong, or that science is fundamentally anti-Christian. Pastors are not generally known for their understanding of complex biological science, so whilst creative and critical analysis is always welcome, casting out the science because it contrasts with one's own particular reading of scripture is a very dangerous – and ultimately fruitless – game.

Yet this appears to be what many church leaders are happy to do. Churches adopt and adore science when it suits their particular needs – we might look only to the recent pandemic to see how much the Church has leaned on the scientific discoveries of radio-waves and vaccines to get through the past two years. Yet when science, which includes both the natural sciences but also the social sciences, challenges religious dogma and doctrine, down comes the drawbridge and out goes any sense of rationality or critical dialogue. To be sure, uncritical reception of every next big thing is no healthier a reaction, and churches (and any institutions) should be wary of ushering in every single scientific development. Yet serious, peer-reviewed, scientific discovery is not something that can be ignored. The more we reject it and make rejection a key part of our faith, the more our faith becomes distant from the world that God made. The more we see faith as being inevitably opposed to the world, the more we run the risk of devastating any chance we might have of mission. A church that refuses to see the world in front of it is a church that is rejecting the very creation it is a part of. A church that ignores phenomena in favour of obtuse abstraction, that fails to recognise and rejoice in real lives, is one that has totally lost its way.

At this stage, it is worth highlighting one key doctrine of the Church that warrants particular attention in any discussion of the importance of experience in discerning the work of the Spirit and the life of God in wider society. The Fall – the doctrine that the world is not as it should be, but rather a place in which disobedience has brought sin and evil – may be expressed in new and different ways in each generation, but nonetheless is a central tenet of the Christian faith. It is because of the Fall – because of the pervasive sin that runs through the life of individuals and communities – that we need grace, and it is because of this need for grace and salvation that Christ died. Such a doctrine is an important corrective to any over-optimistic view of the world, that takes all human experience as good and that ultimately squeezes Christ and salvation out of the narrative of human history. Sin, and our participation in it, is very real to anyone who takes an even cursory glance at human history and at the contemporary world. Any appeal to nature as an absolute good is bound to fail – a topic we shall return to in Chapter 2. Yet the doctrine of the Fall does not inevitably lead to our viewing creation as entirely disordered – it simply calls us to discern carefully where the Spirit is working. The Spirit reveals that which is good, and makes good those things that are in disorder. It is essential that we are open to his work in the world, and in the building up of the Kingdom of God – a Kingdom that is inaugurated, and yet is not brought to completion.

This book calls for a return to dialogue, and to an openness that the Church, and society, desperately need. For us to be in a position where the Church and wider society glare at each other across a river of incomprehension is a travesty. It is a sign of retreat when church leaders resort to appeals to authority, and to a use of religious texts in a way that desecrates and abuses them, rather than uses them in the dance of human dialogue, and show either fear or disdain in their interactions with human knowledge. It is quite extraordinary that some in the Church cannot see that human knowledge is from God – not something to be feared, but something to be celebrated, and journeyed alongside, challenged and be challenged by. As Christians, we carry with us the witness of the ages to the most earth-shattering and remarkable event in human history. The Gospel can take the heat of dialogue. Our theology, like our science, is contingent – our God is not. The more we tie God to our human theology, the more we risk making Him so.

This book also calls for a radical response to the 'problem' that LGBTQI people pose to the Church. It is no longer good enough to see this as something abstract, or as a problem to be solved. We are talking about real people, many of whom are living lives which are abundantly showing the life of the Spirit. The seventh chapter of Matthew's Gospel has plenty to say about judgement and judging others, and one particular line jumps out when we are considering the lives of those who the Church has spent so long criticising, discriminating against and disparaging: Thus you will know them by their fruits (Matthew 7:20). When we hear this line, perhaps we should not only see the 'them' as LGBTQI people – whose good fruits are ever more being recognised and so many of whose lives are so clearly procreative in nature –

31

but also church leaders might see themselves in the 'them' as well. What is the fruit of this discrimination in the name of Christ and his Gospel?

The experience of LGBTQI people says much about not only the vexed question of inclusion, but about the life of the Church itself. In these pages, you will meet some of them – narratives that speak of remarkable devotion to Christ and to his Church, in the face of, in some cases, quite appalling hatred and discrimination. That LGBTQI people continue to go to Church in such numbers is in itself no small miracle. That those who continue to subject them to emotional violence cannot recognise this is inexcusable. Through this book, we will see what the consequences of exclusion, repression, abuse of power and erasure are, for LGBTQI people and for the Church itself – and we will see what a culture of inclusion, expression, openness and joy in being God's people might bring. We will glimpse what a gift LGBTQI people are to God's holy church, and we will begin to sketch out how we might harness that to build up the Kingdom.

The key contention of this book is that for no other significant issue in the life of the Church have 'theological' arguments been made, or succeeded, that so clearly reject overwhelming scientific and experiential knowledge about the human person and human flourishing. We will meet narrative, biopsychosocial research, lived experience, tradition and scripture, and see what God is doing through each of these ways of learning about Him and His people. We will meet challenge and encouragement, hopes and fears – and we will do so alongside God's people of queer holiness, greeting them not as 'other', but as coheirs and as pilgrims on the road to the New Jerusalem.

As much as we might like to think we know it all, no generation has all the answers, and it may be that in centuries, or even in decades, people will look back on this generation as the most arrogant of them all. Yet as human knowledge grows, we have a choice – to hold it up against the refining fire of God's grace, or to reject it and hold on to what is comfortable. Sometimes that which we knew and believed before is of God; sometimes it itself needs refining in the fire. All human knowledge is contingent, as is our theology. Yet God calls out to us in many ways, and we must have ears to hear what the Spirit is saying to the churches in our own time.

2

SO YOU DON'T BELIEVE IN THE BIBLE? PART I

Human beings love certainty. As we have seen over the past few years of the global pandemic, nothing is more discombobulating than a lack of clarity over the future. Some of us may manage the 'not knowing' in a better way than some others, but the reality is that part of the human condition is the desire, and often felt need, to plan, to organise the future, and to avoid as much uncertainty as possible. This is an inevitable part of our evolution as a species: indeed, many of the facets that we now wish we could escape are doubtless parts of our psychological make-up because of our evolutionary history. Not just the psychological, but many of the physical too – for example, a tendency to obesity is almost certainly a result, at least in part, of the need to lay down fat tissue in times of plenty to prepare for times of scarcity.

Humans, then, have spent much of their history adapting behaviour to fit not only their evolutionary heritage, but their context as well. In the modern age, we have medications and procedures to add into our coping strategies, but the underlying problems remain. We are a species that has a history – a history that comes with baggage, physical, psychological, and doubtless spiritual too. Our need for certainty is something we continue to carry with us, even if we try to take steps to avoid it, as is our preference for systematising, for rules and regulations, and for other ways of getting a hold of, and over, our sometimes flighty and never entirely predictable lives. In a world that often tends towards chaos, we have a preference for order, and for interpretations of life that lead to order.

It is no surprise that, both historically and in the present day, much of this desire for order permeates into our religious lives. We can see this throughout the Bible itself – whether in the Deuteronomic Reform under King Josiah[1] or even through the keenness of the Gospel writers to tie in the life of Jesus neatly with predictions or other facets of the Jewish Bible. Systematisation is not a bad thing in itself – without it, it is highly unlikely that the world would have seen anything like the advances in modern technology that have led to thousands of lives saved and living conditions improved. Yet systematisation also lies at the root of many of the world's evils – one need only think of death camps, slavery, and the endless subjugation of peoples through the history of the world to get a glimpse of what systematised evil might look like. For the Christian, then, systematising must be taken into the realm of God and held up in that light – and we must accept that some things are not ours to be certain about. The Book of Job is not an example of theodicy, of explaining evil – it is quite the opposite. Each time we try to systematise God, we run the risk of reducing Him and in so doing, turning our version of Him into an idol, blaspheming against Him and putting ourselves on the heavenly throne. It might sound an obvious thing to avoid, but plenty have made and continue to make that mistake.

It is this need for certainty that sits so uncomfortably with the Bible. This chapter's title is a provocative one, and yet one that is so often thrown at those who hold a positive view of LGBTQI people. 'So you don't believe in the Bible?', we are

---

[1] The Reform is discussed in more detail in Anselm Hagedorn, 'Deuteronomy and the Deuteronomic Reform' in Barmash, P. (ed.), *The Oxford Handbook of Biblical Law* (Oxford: OUP, 2019).

asked, as though that is a simple question to ask. A corollary would be the contrast made between 'Bible believing Christians' – a moniker frequently seen on church websites and literature of a particular bent - and everyone else. Less catchy, but more honest, would be the title 'believers of a particular view of the history, meaning, interpretation and application of the Bible'. It is high time that this kind of self-appointed biblical omniscience – whereby it's 'my way or no way' – is put to bed. The answer of many LGBTQI people to 'do you believe in the Bible' is an unequivocal yes – a yes that is informed by the experience of God in their lives and in finding the words of Scripture speaking to them. Just because their interpretation is different to others' doesn't mean they don't believe or that they don't place the Bible above everything else in their lives. Indeed, quite often their way of reading the Bible shows it more respect, rather than less, because it takes the Bible on its own terms, and doesn't ask it to do what it is not able to do, nor designed to do. The Bible is not an instruction manual.

The authority of the Bible is not something that is up for question in any serious discussion of Christian theology, and anyone who tries to convince you otherwise is either being dishonest or does not understand that of which they speak. Yet there are serious, intelligent questions to ask about what we mean by 'authority', and about how we see the Bible interact and dialogue with other parts of human life. There are a number of threads, however, that have run throughout Christian history, and we are foolish to ignore them.

In the first instance, it has always been a fundamental facet of Christian belief that Jesus Christ is the Word of God – the *logos*, consubstantial with the Father. In recent years, there has been a surfeit of literature that speaks of the Bible as the Word of God instead. On this, we must be very careful indeed. Most Christians would agree that the Bible is, indeed, divinely inspired – yet would also recognise that it was written, under this inspiration, by human hand. The Bible, unlike the Quran and some other holy books, is not believed to have been dictated by God through a human conduit. As such, it is not the Word of God (for such a title is reserved to Christ) – although it may be the word of God, as we frequently repeat in the liturgy. This does not devalue it, or suggest less respect – instead, it reminds us that as Christians we are oriented to God through the Bible and not the other way around.[2]

The Bible is a divinely-inspired record of God's revelation, through the patriarchs and prophets, and ultimately through the life, death and resurrection of Jesus Christ, the Word made flesh. Jesus Christ is definitive – the Bible is a record of that revelation. We do not and must not worship the Bible, even if we do reverence it as pointing towards God. It is holy because it brings us closer to the creator of the universe, and it is how God has chosen to reveal Himself.

Yet the Bible is not simple. It is not a history book, or a set of rules and regulations, or simply a work of theology, although it contains each of those genres and more. Ultimately, it is a narrative formed from a number of documents of a whole host of genres that in its entirety points to the salvation of humankind. It is a record of God's self-revelation, and of the journeying of humankind alongside our Lord and saviour. It is remarkable in its breadth and in its ability to speak from particular contexts into those throughout Christian history and our own. It is scandalous in its particularity and yet also astonishing in its wide applicability and relevance.

For some, however, the lack of simplicity is seen as a threat rather than a gift. Seen through the lens of our need to have control and certainty, we can begin to see why this might be the case. God's revelation, however much we might try, is always going to just escape our systematising, however clever our systematic theologians. We know, from serious biblical scholarship, how complicated the history

---

[2] Different denominations will emphasise this point in different ways, but the central distinction between word and Word is found throughout historical and contemporary Christian teaching. Interested readers may wish to consult *Dei Verbum* (a key document of the Second Vatican Council). Debates on the finer details of this topic continue in biblical studies literature to date.

of the stitching together of the biblical canon is, and how many questions remain unanswered.[3] Gone are the days in which anyone in academia would take seriously the idea that Moses wrote the Pentateuch, or that the books of the Bible are in chronological order. It is outside the scope of this book to delve more into the specifics of biblical historical scholarship, but it is not acceptable for theologians to inhabit a cognitive dissonance whereby we know one thing about the way the Bible was written and yet when we read it with the eyes of faith we ignore that very history. It has become abundantly clear that the Bible, contrary to so many pronouncements from within the Church, is not nearly as clear about a whole host of issues as simplistic preachers might want us to believe.

We must take far more seriously in our preaching what we know in our academic lives. Preachers are still far too often heard expounding on a passage of scripture in a way that totally ignores the last century of serious academic research; research that fundamentally changes how that passage ought to be understood, and what the original purpose of that passage was. Not only do we know that the Bible's provenance is complicated, but we should also recognise quite how contextual these texts are. When we read the Epistles, for example, and expect a fully worked-through theology for all circumstances and for all time within them, we are being disingenuous both to the Bible and to its human authors. We need to meet the Bible where it is at, and read its pages in a way that recognises its own contingency and context, however divinely inspired. To return to the theme, it is Jesus Christ, revealed through the words of scripture and continuing to live amongst us, who is definitive. The Bible may indeed speak to us in our own contexts, but if we ignore its original and various contexts, we do it, and the Christian faith, a monstrous disservice.

---

[3] Readers may enjoy exploring this question – and several of those raised in this chapter – in Barton, J., *A History of the Bible* (London: Penguin, 2019).

It is not only preachers who hold this responsibility, but those who attend our churches as well. It is unacceptable for churchgoers to turn up to church and (often through the encouragement of pastors) leave their brains at the door. In the daily lives of many Christians, hugely complex decisions must be made, which rely on the whole gamut of human knowledge, discovery and critical thought. It is astounding that we so often fail to apply our critical faculties to our faith, and instead are willing to imbibe deeply flawed and fundamentally unsupportable readings of scripture, simply because it is more comfortable to do so. 'The Bible is very clear' is a phrase which must be used extremely sparingly, if at all – and certainly less than many of our churches do today. This is not an arrogant raising of the human intellect above the words of the Bible – it is a call to utilise the gift of human intellect to show proper respect to the word of God. If we are willing to use our critical faculties in making money, or in analysing the world around us, why are we so frequently loathe to do it in church?

Of course, too much critical thought can cause all kinds of trouble. The Reformers, having argued against the monopoly of the clergy to read, let alone interpret the Bible, came up against this difficulty. The Roman Catholic Church has its magisterium, offering an interpretation of scripture that is definitive for the worldwide church. For a church that prizes order, not least to avoid heresy in such a huge global communion, such an approach certainly has its advantages. Yet for a magisterium to be effective, it also has to be responsive and open to genuine, serious challenge. The experience of the Roman Catholic Church over the past several hundred years – if not longer – is that such a challenge is neither welcome nor tolerated. The Holy Office – now redubbed the Congregation for the Doctrine of the Faith – has not covered itself in glory through the years, has managed to oppose many things which have later been quietly accepted, and has not been known as an encourager of diverse opinion.[4] Some might argue that it simply takes time for the Roman Catholic Church to move on matters of doctrine – the frequently heard refrain that the Church moves in centuries and that it is God's time and not human time that matters. The holiness of such a refrain is, however, doubtful when teenagers continue to kill themselves because the Church continues to call them intrinsically disordered.

If the Roman church is not to solidify under the weight of its own intransigence, then some serious reform of doctrinal decision making is surely in order. The work of Jesuit author James Martin[5] has done some of the heavy lifting in this regard, but too often it appears that warm words disguise a brick wall. Meanwhile, behind that wall are real people losing their faith and losing their lives. Handwringing by those who privately want change does not cut the mustard. In 2013, the Pope was congratulated for replying to a question from a journalist by saying 'if a person is gay and seeks God and has good will, who am I to judge?'. The more pertinent question for an institution that continues to actively discriminate against LGBTQI people, in its structures and in its actions, is perhaps – how will I be judged, as universal pastor? It seems unlikely that it will be gay teenagers placed under the judgement of God.

Returning to the Reformers, the key question that needed to be asked after the rejection of the Magisterium was – so how do we interpret the scriptures?[6] As opposed to clericalism as Luther was, the intention was not to create a free-for-all, in which any interpretation was deemed correct. In the contemporary world, we hear much – often disparagingly from political commentators of a certain hue – about 'my truth', as opposed to 'the truth'. This is the risk of

[4] One need think only about its genesis in 1542 (under the official title *The Supreme Sacred Congregation of the Roman and Universal Inquisition*), where it was founded by Pope Paul III to seek out and condemn 'errors' and 'false doctrines', and its role in propagating the *Index Librorum Prohibitorum* (the List of Prohibited Books).

[5] For example, Martin, J., *Building a Bridge* (San Francisco: HarperOne, 2018)

[6] A specific Anglican discussion can be found in Avis, P., *In Search of Authority* (London: Bloomsbury Academic, 2014).

any opening up of what was previously closely guarded, and yet a relativised world-view is not the inevitable outcome of such a liberalisation.

The Church of England, primarily through the three-legged stool often associated with Richard Hooker,[7] came to an understanding that Scripture, Tradition and Reason all contribute to the life of faith, and hence all play a part in the dance of ecclesial authority. Whilst scripture is properly seen as the leg with the greatest importance, nonetheless each of these threads interacted with, dialogued with and enhanced the other. To that end, the heart of Anglicanism as an idea and as an ecclesiology, as it has developed through time, has never been one in which the Bible has been asked to do for believers what it is not able and not gifted to do. The Bible is a dialogue partner – the senior partner, indeed, but a partner nonetheless. The Church of England takes the ongoing revelation of God through history very seriously indeed – the Bible is indeed complete, but the work of the Spirit is not, and the Bible can point us to where that work continues in our own day.

John Wesley gave a further gift to this dance by including experience (described as 'the inner witness of the Spirit') alongside scripture, tradition and reason in what has come to be known as the Wesleyan Quadrilateral.[8] Whilst Wesley is primarily associated with the Methodist Church – a denomination which, in the UK at least, has finally applied this quadrilateral to issues of sex and gender and recognised the gift of God in LGBTQI people in recent years – as an ordained Church of England clergyman, he has much to tell us. Wesley, much like Hooker, believed in *prima scriptura* – the

[7] The association with Richard Hooker is contested – for a discussion, see for example Estes, J., *Anglican Manifesto* (Eugene: Wipf and Stock, 2014) and Chapman, M., *Anglican Theology* (London: Bloomsbury Publishing, 2012). A wider discussion of the three-legged stool and its relationship to sexuality is found in Thatcher, A., *God, Sex, and Gender* (London: Wiley, 2011) pp. 34-40.
[8] For a discussion, see Ted A. Campbell, 'Authority and the 'Wesleyan Quadrilateral' in Yrigoyen Jr, C. (ed.), *T&T Clark Companion to Methodism* (London: Bloomsbury T&T Clark, 2014), pp.61-72.

primacy of Scripture – but he also recognised how each of the other dialogue partners were essential if the Bible were to be truly honoured. Whilst some might now argue against the somewhat simplistic nature of Wesley's description of experience – his famous phrase 'what the scriptures promise, I enjoy' feeling somewhat optimistic when held up against the ravages of history, and his argument that we must experience something personally to have assurance of it – nonetheless his contribution to the theological debate is invaluable. In many ways, experience and reason are two sides of the same coin – reason is, in essence, reflection on experience, which makes use of critical faculties and joins the anecdotal and personal to the evidenced and generalisable. It is in this vein that we might reinterpret Hooker for the post-Enlightenment age.

The final of the three dialogue partners, tradition, is the one that is perhaps the least popular in the present age. The contemporary world has quite the hermeneutic of suspicion towards tradition – it has far too often been seen as a tool of oppression and privilege rather than as protection against the worst excesses of human tyranny. Tradition is where the Magisterium of the Roman Catholic Church sits, whilst in churches that are both Reformed and Catholic, like the Church of England, tradition is somewhat harder to define. A simple, though inadequate, description might be those inherited and yet still living threads of faith that retain the good and guard against those things that might diminish the Christian faith and the Christian life. Examples in the Church of England might be the Book of Common Prayer, the celebration of the Holy Eucharist, and the Elizabethan Settlement.[9]

Yet beyond these more formal examples, there are

[9] In brief, a set of religious and political decisions that attempted to end religious turmoil in the wake of the Reformation. For example, they included the conferral of the title Supreme Governor of the Church of England on Queen Elizabeth I, the reintroduction of the Book of Common Prayer and the adoption of the Thirty-Nine Articles. For a discussion see Maltby, J., *Prayer Book and People in Elizabethan and Early Stuart England* (Cambridge: CUP, 1998).

more ephemeral, although no less important, factors that contribute to our tradition – the importance of tolerance, of being a broad church, of being a church for the whole nation and a presence in each community. Any religious institution carries within it the inherited wisdom and practices of preceding ages, and part of the role of any age is to sift that tradition for the good, and to cast away the bad or outdated. Arguments continue, of course, about what is central to the tradition, and what is peripheral, and whilst some hoping to modernise the Church might argue that they aren't interested in tradition, what they are really doing is making choices about which part of the tradition they most value. Those who argue that things cannot change simply have different priorities.

If we recognise that we need to apply reason to our theology as a gift of God in creation, then we need to ask what we are looking for in holy scripture. Christ Himself offers us the hermeneutical key – a wonderful example of the Bible interpreting itself (Matthew 22:36-40):

> 'Teacher, which commandment in the law is the greatest?' He said to him, '"You shall love the Lord your God with all your heart, and with all your soul, and with all your mind." This is the greatest and first commandment. And a second is like it: "You shall love your neighbour as yourself." On these two commandments hang all the law and the prophets.'

This is a key passage in biblical interpretation, not least because of the propensity of so many preachers to either misinterpret or plainly ignore it. In the first instance, it is important not to fall into the trap of repeating blithe broad-brush, yet ultimately lazy, clichés that run along the lines of 'God is love and God loves everything'. The former statement is biblical; the latter most certainly is not. It is not a valid Christian theology that refuses to grapple with biblical prohibitions and commendations, and instead wishes to stir them all into a soup of 'anything goes'. Scripture is commonly uncomfortable, and we cannot simply ignore those parts we don't like as if they don't exist. To do so is not only appalling scholarship; it is blasphemy.

Yet that is not the same as saying every line of the Bible is the same in terms of weight that should be given it, or how it applies in the modern day. It has never been the case, through the entire history of Christian and Jewish scholarship and faith practice, and indeed in the Bible's interpretation of itself, that every line of scripture is of the same nature. St Paul tells us (Romans 15:4) that 'whatever was written in former days was written for our instruction, so that by steadfastness and by the encouragement of the scriptures we might have hope', and it is this pronouncement that is most helpful to us when we are reading the words of the Bible. We have already seen the wide array of different genres found in the Bible, from poetry to theology, religious history to proverbial sayings, and each must be taken on its own terms and read with an eye to its context. It is the steadfastness and encouragement of the scriptures that give us hope – and such hope requires us to read, mark, learn and inwardly digest them (as the Book of Common Prayer tells us). It also requires us to constantly keep in mind our own biases and hold any interpretative methodology up against the Scriptures themselves.

Ultimately, the hermeneutical key is Christ Himself. That Christ comes to fulfil the law rather than abolish it is surely a key tenet of the Christian faith (Matthew 5:17), and the Bible – through the letters of St Paul, St James and elsewhere – itself offers a meditation on what this fulfilment looks like. It is not only by what Christ says that we can begin to glimpse the salvation of the world, but by who he is and what he does. It is notable that in the creeds of the Church catholic, very little is said about Jesus's words *per se* – much more is said about what his life, entire and complete, means. Joining words with action is perhaps most clearly seen in the farewell dialogue in St John's Gospel (John 13:34-5):

'I give you a new commandment, that you love one another. Just as I have loved you, you also should love one another. By this everyone will know that you are my disciples, if you have love for one another.'

This is not some form of wishy-washy or insipid love – Christ is soon to be betrayed, denied, deserted and crucified, and yet he 'loved them to the end' (John 13:1). Here, we see Jesus pointing to his very life as the fulfilment of the law and the prophets – he is embodied love – loving both God and neighbour in unity. It is this love of God and neighbour that sums up everything the prophets and law have declared, and it is this that is the core of the Gospel and of God's revelation to humankind. The law and the prophets, the theology and the poetry, the proverbs and the revealed history – all of this, found in the Bible and in the lives of God's people, point to that core. God's love is fierce, and refining; it makes demands, rejoicing in the good and rejecting the evil. It is within this core that human flourishing is surely enveloped. Jesus Christ – true God and true man – the embodiment of human flourishing in the way of God.

3

SO YOU DON'T BELIEVE IN THE BIBLE? PART II

When we look to the scriptures for guidance on human flourishing, then, we must always and constantly look towards this core. Any focus on the periphery at the expense of the core of the Gospel will surely lead us astray. When we look at any human situation, or at an episode recalled in the scriptures, this must always be our first thought – where is the core of the Gospel at work here? Where are the commandments of God?

> The Pharisees and the scribes asked him, 'Why do your disciples not live according to the tradition of the elders, but eat with defiled hands?' He said to them, 'Isaiah prophesied rightly about you hypocrites, as it is written,
>
> "This people honours me with their lips,
> but their hearts are far from me;
> in vain do they worship me,
> teaching human precepts as doctrines."
>
> You abandon the commandment of God and hold to human tradition.'
>
> (Mark 7:5-8)

Many a superficial reading of this passage has led to a general condemnation of tradition and all it entails – and at the worst excesses of this kind of thinking, it has led to a total rejection of Jewish law and practice. Yet with some nuance and balance, it doesn't appear that this is what Jesus is saying. Jesus is not condemning the Jewish law – together with all of its precepts, requirements, ritual elements – but he is reminding his disciples what the law is for – where the law is supposed to point. The things in themselves are not the centre of the faith or its fulfilment – the traditions are there to serve human flourishing, and not the other way around. Jesus is by no means condemning tradition *per se* – but he is reminding us that tradition for its own sake is empty and in fact may simply turn us into hypocrites.

This is the standard against which we must hold any attempt we might make to conserve things, or to hold on to tradition. It is also the standard we must use when interpreting the scriptures. Are we focusing on the centre or the periphery when we dialogue with passages of scripture? Are we conserving the peripheries – are the out-workings of underlying principles becoming more important than the principles themselves? Are we conserving the human tinkerings around the edges, or the thing itself? Are we, in fact, conserving the superficial at the expense of the thing of substance that should be at the heart of it?

It was in such a spirit that Pope St John XXIII called the Second Vatican Council, with a call to *aggiornamento* – bringing up to date – coupled with *ressourcement* – a return to the sources.[1] This approach ran a coach and horses through the liberal-conservative binary – it threw out the contemporary wisdom that progress meant throwing out the past, and that this posed a threat to the survival of the Church. It was, instead, a return to the teaching of Jesus, itself

---

[1] A detailed discussion of these concepts and their relevance to the Second Vatican Council is found in O'Collins, G., *The Second Vatican Council: Message and Meaning* (Collegeville: Liturgical Press, 2014).

demanding a total change in our orientation away from the periphery and into the centre. It sits uncomfortably in our contemporary society, refusing as it does to be simple and binary.

We may, indeed, find that that which is most 'progressive' may itself be most conservative as well – conserving the things that matter and that sit at the heart of our faith and at the heart of human flourishing. This is why the word 'radical' is so important to the Christian life. Radical – from radix, for root – is surely how Christians must live out the faith – from the root, finding those kernels of value that are embedded in the heart of God and which set the people of God free to live, love, worship and flourish.

Many a self-identified secular conservative political commentator over the ages has poured scorn on liberation movements – whether black lives matter, or the struggle for women's suffrage, or LGBTQI rights, or the rights of prisoners and refugees. These things are too radical, we are told – they will tear down society, and we need to conserve what we have. Yet such campaigns, if they are truly radical, are themselves often conserving the thing that really matters – human dignity. There is no simple definition for a conservative, because what we choose to conserve matters. In the Church, those who speak proudly of conserving or of having 'conservative' readings of scripture must be challenged – what are you conserving and what is at the core of this conservation? Are you truly conserving the good, or are you abandoning the commandment of God and holding to human tradition and the peripheries of life instead? Are you conserving those things that give life, or those things that encase human life in an immovable edifice?

It is for this reason that proof texting is such a bad idea. This practice – now frowned upon by even some self-proclaimed conservatives – is one in which particular Bible verses or passages are taken out of context and utilised as texts with which to bash one's opponents over the head. Examples in the LGBTQI sphere would be Leviticus 18:22 or various passages (and particular translations thereof) in St Paul's epistles. To totally ignore context – both the immediate context of the passage but also the wider context of to whom the passage is written and its original author's perspective and aim – is not a mature way of handling scripture, yet it remains one that far too often raises its head in contemporary debates. Picking and choosing particular passages, rather than respecting the internal integrity of scripture, is dangerous – not least because it dares to suggest that the exegete's selection has more to say than the totality of the inspired word of God.

To avoid proof-texting is not to say that the Bible is 'wrong' – it is to appeal to a hermeneutic that looks to the overarching narrative of scripture rather than simplistic notions built on particular texts (and one that attempts to identify and name any assumptions we might make in our reading of the text). It is well-known that scripture contradicts itself in places (one need only think of the variable order of creation in Genesis 1 and 2), but this is not to call scripture false. Indeed, the truth of scripture is a narrative truth about humanity, reaching its culmination in the story of Jesus Christ, true God and true man. To view scripture through this lens is not to say that the interpreter knows more than the authors – or indeed, Jesus Himself. Instead, this is a very high view of scripture indeed – not a high view of the individual authors *per se*, but a high view of the God who reveals Himself. A thoughtful, reflective process of reading scripture, utilising all the tools human knowledge has gifted us, is anything but an insult to the creator of the universe. To deny that we need discernment when reading the Bible, however, is to obfuscate and deny contradiction and difficulty. There is no single way to read the Bible, and there is no certainty – yet this contingency has always been how humans have faced their God, and it is a radical discontinuity with the entire human experience to deny this.

Proof texting, taken to its natural conclusion, leads to a place in which our focus turns to the periphery and not to the core Gospel message. In the LGBTQI sphere, churches continue to spend far too long focusing on acts themselves rather than recognising acts as representative of something far more important and integral to the human condition. In the next two chapters, we will delve into this area further, but if we read the Bible as an instruction manual that talks primarily about what we do rather than about what we are, we are bound to run into significant difficulties. Of course, what we do matters – the intention to steal, for example, is problematical because it points towards our thoughts, desires, and ontology, but if we do not steal despite the urge, particularly if this comes from a place of faith and intentional self-denial, then we somewhat counter the evil. But a focus on the externals here would not be on stealing, but on taking that for which we have not paid – an act that may come from a whole host of internal dispositions with their own sets of reasons. To focus on that external act does not do justice to the ontology – it ignores the human person and solely points towards (often erroneously interpreted) physical manifestations. Reading the Bible in a way that is driven entirely by the externals rather than the interior life is a reading that focuses on the peripherals and not the core.

This is where so much 'biblical' theology ends up.[2] A focus on a literalist, peripherally-focused reading of scripture leads to us believing God's own attention is on the external and not the internal – quite in contrast to the vision of God to which the Bible itself attests. In matters of sexuality, the key proof texts (often referred to as the 'clobber texts') focus primarily on sex between men. This raises a number of questions. First, there are significant questions to be raised where what appears to be condemnation of genital acts between two

---

[2] And why the terms 'Bible believing' or 'Bible based', when used by particular churches or political factions as weapons or as ways to denigrate opponents, are so toxic. Nobody has ownership of the Bible except God, and to use it in this way is blasphemous. We may differ in our interpretations, but it is fundamentally unacceptable to claim to possess the Bible in this way.

men becomes the key text of judgement on all homosexual love and activity. Many 'conservative' commentators will tell us that because the Bible clearly [sic] condemns genital acts between men, it must follow that lesbianism is also strictly forbidden. We are bound to make reference to Romans 1:26-27 here as a classic example of a clobber text that may refer to some form of 'genital acts' between women, although its meaning remains much contested (not least given no reference to same-sex female sexuality in the Old Testament) and it is once again primarily focused on male sexuality (and here too the meaning remains contested). It is a shame that so many anti-LGBTQI commentators suspend their cultural and contextual understanding when reading such texts, yet apply a generalised approach when they have determined their meaning – seeing this as relating to same-sex activity *per se*, and then condemning all same-sex activity as a consequence. We get, then, to a place in which relationships which are not mentioned whatsoever in the Bible are condemned on extremely flimsy grounds.

That is not to mention the huge debates that rage – as much as certain commentators would like to pretend that they don't – about the meaning of the words commonly, and many would argue erroneously, translated or interpreted to refer to consensual homosexual activity. It is by no means clear that the overarching biblical narrative is one that condemns (or even considers) consensual homosexual activity – the discussion of which is outside the scope of this book, but can be found amongst more serious biblical exegetes of many different stripes.[3] Yet even if particular texts are indeed referring to situations that are equivalent to consensual, homosexual acts in the context of what would be considered a contemporary relationship, it is not enough to

---

[3] Readers will likely want to explore this discussion in more detail than that presented here. It is recommended that a variety of authors – from various different angles – are consulted. As much as some commentators might wish to argue, there is no single settled view on this issue, not least because any interpretation comes with inevitable implicit biases.

simply point to isolated texts without engaging with the whole record of God's revelation, through scripture and through scripture applied to and tested against the living history of the people of God. To expect the Bible to be definitive on this particular question, and not on other specific contemporary discussions which are not even conceived of in the pages of holy scripture, is bizarre.

We do not expect a specific biblical position on the stock market, for example – instead, we comb the pages of scripture and try to discern the mind of God through scripture, tradition and reason. It is quite inexplicable that some exegetes refuse to do so in the context of contemporary homosexual relationships. Maybe it comes back to our insatiable demand for certainty where there is none. We may posit that there is one single biblical position on same-sex love, or even on love and sex in general – we may state *ad nauseam* that the Bible is 'perfectly clear', but it quite simply isn't true. It would be much better for us to seek out the deeper meaning of scripture and to recognise that it is in its integrity and in its whole that it speaks to human situations, rather than try to turn the Bible into something that it is not. Our desire for – and arrogant claim to have found – certainty has a lot to answer for.

It is important to reiterate that God does not bless everything, and this includes things in the area of sex, sexuality and relationships. The biblical record in this regard is genuinely clear: God does not bless abusive relationships, does not bless the subjugation of women, does not bless infidelity and does not bless coercive sexual behaviour. The Bible is clear in this regard because the entire canon of scripture points in this direction – through books of different genres, eras and audiences. Yet the Bible has a lot to say about the importance of honesty, of commitment, of love and of fidelity. It also has much material that commends human beings as embodied and relational. These facets appear to be the core of the Bible's teaching on relationships, and it is to this that the peripheral discussions point. It is quite simply not clear that the possibility for such monogamous, sexual relationships are restricted to opposite sex couples – most particularly when experience is taken into account (as we shall see in following chapters). In short, the Bible appears to be more interested in where people put their hearts, rather than their genitalia.

The problem with refusing to meet the Bible on its own terms is that we ultimately turn it into an idol. It rather surprisingly comes as a shock to many Christians, but it is the Church which preceded the Bible and not the other way around. The canon of scripture was not finalised until several centuries into the Christian era, and the historical record suggests that the creeds, or at least a version of them, may have preceded at least the formal recognition of the canon. It is because of this that we cannot simply see the Bible as a standalone book – as we have seen, it is of its culture, of its context, and it is of the Church. That is not to deny the role of the Holy Spirit in guiding the councils of the Church and in forming the canon, but it is simply perverse denial to refuse to recognise its enmeshed relationship with the Church.

It is because of this relationship that we must seriously consider the role of tradition when we read, interpret, and use the Bible. One helpful word when considering the role of tradition is 'witness'. The word is a theme for the writer of Luke and Acts, and at the end of Luke's Gospel (Chapter 24:48), we hear Jesus tell the disciples 'you are witnesses of these things'. Tradition is a living repository of this witness, and rather than see the Bible as static, our role as the Church today means that the dialogue between living tradition and scripture continues. To turn the Bible into a fossil of the past is to devalue it – it is God's gift to the Church and the world, and our being witnesses means looking not only from the Bible into the world but from the world into the Bible as well. It is by doing so that we are able to hold in tension the completed nature of the Bible and yet its relevance to every age and time.

At this point, it is important to highlight the sheer variety of ways that the scriptures have been interpreted when it comes to LGBTQI people and their relationships. Some of these interpretations have more merit than others, but it is nonetheless true that exegetes have come to the same Bible and come away with fundamentally differing positions on what the Bible says, some more contingent than others. Many of these views are deeply held – although there does seem to be a preponderance of non-LGBTQI people who hold views that argue against the liberation of LGBTQI people. Such views are, it is arguable, rather easier to hold when there is no personal experience or direct effect felt – and as we shall see in Part II of this book, the cognitive dissonance caused by the holding of these views amongst those who feel unable to express themselves as LGBTQI can often have devastating consequences.

Nonetheless, there do appear to be some appropriate ways of interpreting scripture, and some inappropriate, if the measure is the history of Christian thought and discipleship. It is the premise of this chapter, and this book more generally, that any exegesis that rejects experience and reason out of hand is ultimately dishonest – and un-biblical. The Bible itself is a narrative, and thus by its very nature lends validity to the use of experience in discerning the work and movement of the Holy Spirit. If experience, discovery and reason all oppose particular interpretations of scripture, then at the very least these interpretations need to be interrogated and likely refined. As we have seen, a theology – described as biblical or otherwise – that rejects the overwhelming evidence on human flourishing is hard to defend when held up against the tenets of the Christian faith.

One key question to be asked, having considered all this, is whether the Bible really has anything to say whatsoever about what a healthy LGBTQI life should look like. The answer to this is both yes and no. It is abundantly clear from biblical scholarship that the Bible doesn't specifically refer to what we would now recognise as healthy same-sex relationships. Yet on the other hand, the central, core message of the Gospel has much to say to human beings in relationship – including, it can be argued, contemporary same-sex couples, created in the image of God and redeemed by Christ to be a new creation. It is not clear, then, that we should immediately move from 'the Bible says nothing about consensual, contemporary, monogamous same-sex relationships' to 'therefore such relationships are un-biblical'. That is surely to throw the baby out with the bathwater, and to refuse to open our eyes to the work of the Spirit. It is to arbitrarily restrict the recipients of the Good News, and that is not a job for human beings – quite the opposite. That the Bible doesn't specifically refer to contemporary same-sex relationships is a reflection of its cultural context – it is hardly a valid argument to suggest that because scripture is not positive about same sex relationships, then all such relationships are condemned by omission.

It is much simpler, of course, to demand that there is only one interpretation of scripture – one that has been consistent and thus cannot be changed. Not only is this a misreading of the historical reality, but it is a very brave human being that decides that their view is the only possible one. In recent years, there has been an increase in the number of theologies that arise in the periphery rather than the centre of what might traditionally be seen to be church structures. These include the various liberation theologies, feminist, womanist, black, disabled, queer and other theologies that are embedded in the experience of those pushed to the margins of society and the Church. Far too often, these are contrasted with 'biblical' theologies, which are marketed as the real thing compared to these 'radical' and even 'dangerous' disrupters. It is time to put that kind of talk to bed. Jesus – in the Bible – points to the periphery as the place where the Gospel is often found but too rarely sought by the comfortable centre ground. The periphery of the Church and society are perhaps key to identifying the core of the Gospel message. These theologies may be contingent, but so is all human understanding, biblical or otherwise.

It is to these human experiences that we now turn, with a call to the Church to open its ears and eyes to those on the margins. The world – God's world – has much to say about human flourishing, and it is time we paid attention.

4

LIFE IN ALL ITS FULLNESS
PART I

C hurch debates on the life and loves of LGBTQI people have far too often discussed 'issues' in the abstract, rather than shown much recognition that such discussions are about real people. A particular challenge comes when proponents of a 'conservative' or 'traditional' viewpoint – words which must always be disputed and challenged, as we discussed in Chapter 2 – claim a false equivalence between the hurt that they feel when their views are challenged, and the utterly incomparable damage that is done to LGBTQI people when their entire sense of self, identity and personhood is trampled underfoot. To have one's theological position disputed, threatened, and even insulted, is frustrating and even upsetting, although such arguments are always best met with arguments rather than an appeal to one's hurt feelings. Yet this is fundamentally of a different nature to the onslaught that LGBTQI people have been subject to throughout history, in which their very selves are held up and found to be unworthy of the love of God. Of course, those who oppose LGBTQI freedoms would say that, in the main, they oppose the acts and not the person themselves – the old line 'hate the sin, love the sinner' coming into its own – and what they are desperate to do is to save the sinner from the punishment for their sin. That said, there is still enough in the polemic and even serious academic discussion from opponents of LGBTQI people that doesn't quite suggest this is the case – the words 'intrinsically disordered' are not yet a thing of history.[1]

The phrase 'hate the sin, love the sinner' also belies a deep current of dualism that runs through much of the anti-LGBTQI lobby's theological posturing. If that view is to be taken on its own terms, then we are led to an understanding of the human being that runs far too strong a line between a person's acts and their ontology. Not only is this entirely counter to the entire history of Christian thought on embodiment and human wholeness,[2] but it also flies in the face of contemporary understandings of the body as well. It is deeply flawed to imagine that one's being – which includes sexual desire, and longing for relationship – is entirely separate from acting on such feelings, and we know from basic psychological knowledge that being prevented from acting on some of the most human of feelings – most particularly when this is enforced rather than freely chosen – is detrimental to mental health (and even physical health) and indeed to the ability of individuals to play their full part in society. Worse still is the total repression of one's thoughts – the denial of even thinking a particular way, let alone acting upon it.[3] Yet this has been the modus for the Church

---

[1]   Indeed, this phrase is still found in the Catechism of the Roman Catholic Church, paragraph 2357.

[2]   Much has been written in this area in recent years – not least in relation to worship – and it is interesting to note the Gnostic themes that often arise when mind-body separation is overemphasised. A useful contribution in this area is found in Sigurdson, O., *Heavenly Bodies: Incarnation, the Gaze, and Embodiment in Christian Theology* (Grand Rapids: Eerdmans, 2016) – in which the themes of individual and corporate embodiment throughout human history are discussed.

[3]   The psychological literature here is rich and varied, with a number of different explanatory theories, but the empirical data points in the same direction. It appears common in works of theology to pick and choose particular studies to support one's assertions (a key example would be the selective use of non-theological sources in arguments put forward in Robert Gagnon's *The Bible and Homosexual Practice* (Nashville: Abingdon, 2001)), which can easily lead to an erroneous understanding of the wider literature.

for far too long in its demands on LGBTQI people.

Of course, not all desires, sexual or otherwise, are good. There are a number of examples that we might point to as thoughts, the manifestations of which would certainly do harm, either to the individual concerned or to others. It is at least partly for this reason that we have the Mental Health Act in the United Kingdom, and it is why those who have particular destructive thoughts or feelings are encouraged to seek help – and from a Christian perspective, we might argue are obliged to. There remain cases – for example those unable to feel empathy or those with particular neurobiological conditions that make such decision-making very challenging – where culpability for actions is not black and white, and society has determined methods of trying to meet these challenges, amongst them concepts of consent and capacity.[4] Yet nonetheless, most people have a choice – albeit not a totally free one – as to whether to act on particular feelings, and the choice they make is not unidirectional. A choice to act or not to act will ultimately feed back into those thoughts and feelings, either strengthening or weakening them, and affecting the psychological make-up of the individual. It is not as simple as acting or not acting – the actions (and lack of them) have significant consequences for the individual, and to ignore these is to construct a two-dimensional form of human life that cannot possibly engage with a serious inquiry into human flourishing.

At this stage, it is useful to focus on the concept of

Instead, the author recommends any interested reader to delve into the psychological literature to discover more about this topic, paying particular attention to articles and books that review the literature as a whole. A key starting point for general readers might be Burke, P. (ed.), *Contemporary Social Psychological Theories* (Stanford: Stanford University Press, 2006), Davey, G. C., *Psychology* (London: Wiley, 2018) or for a slightly older text that specifically covers theories of repression, see Singer, J. (ed.), *Repression and Dissociation* (Chicago: University of Chicago Press, 1995).

[4] We might think of those described as 'psychopaths' or those who have had particular brain injuries that affect the pre-frontal lobes of the brain. An interesting discussion of empathy is found in Decety, J., and Ickes, W., eds., *The Social Neuroscience of Empathy* (Boston: MIT, 2009).

'acts' in human sexuality, a topic that is infrequently given the serious consideration it deserves. At first glance, the prohibition on sexual activity between people of the same sex appears relatively simple yet delving into it we begin to recognise its intangibility. Whilst recently the rather inelegant phrase 'genital acts' has become one of the key descriptions of what is forbidden, there is a lot in the grey area between such 'genital acts' and platonic friendship. As we noted in Chapters 2 and 3, much of the prohibition is focused on male genitalia, and much church dialogue appears to suggest that the only form of sexual contact between people is penetrative intercourse. That this remains the nexus of the argument highlights another key problem with silo theology that ignores the wider culture and context – we end up discussing topics at a level which portrays our ignorance of any external developments, and indeed that is ultimately pedestrian and so outdated as to be embarrassing.

Of course, penetrative intercourse has never been the sole form of sexual expression – and it is arguable that it hasn't even been the primary form. Secular discussions on sexuality and sex have not moved towards wider discussions of sex because sexual expression has so fundamentally changed – although of course the sexual revolution has perhaps enabled more people to think of the fun of sex as being something worth considering. The prime change in societal terms has been the increased openness of individuals to talk about sex – to think about what does and does not arouse them, what they would like in terms of sexual practice rather than what they are expected to do by society, and with whom they might want to express themselves sexually. Key beneficiaries of this greater openness have been women and, more recently, non-binary people – and movements such as #MeToo have highlighted how pervasive non-consensual, coercive sexual acts remain. The societal benefit of this openness is clear to see, and the hidden tragedies of sexual exploitation and misery in unfulfilled sexual lives are slowly coming out into the open, offering opportunities for these terrible realities to be addressed and redressed. A society that pretends that all sex is consensual penetrative sex between man and wife that is oriented towards childbearing is a society that lets down its most vulnerable, and one that allows prudishness to get in the way of human safety, let alone human flourishing. If we are to protect others, then sex needs to stop being a dirty word. Society appears rather further ahead in this regard than the Church, although there is still much to do.

Given what we now know about sexual expression, it is extremely difficult to delineate that which is sensual from that which is sexual, if we are committed to an acts-based set of rules as to what is and is not acceptable. It is here that the question – 'so what exactly do you mean by gay sex?' – is so pertinent. Those arguing for LGBTQI equality have frequently been accused of deliberately trying to derail conversations about sexuality when asking this question, but it is not those who celebrate LGBTQI people who are advocating for an acts-based approach. It is not surprising that it is challenging to separate out the sexual and the sensual in terms of acts – every human activity is imbued with meaning that takes account of its context and culture, of intention, audience and recipient. One person's platonic kiss may be another person's sexual kiss – it is not, with some exceptions, the act that by itself declares what is happening to be sexual, but rather everything that is imbued within it. This is a key gift from the social sciences to discussions on relationships and sexuality, yet it is one that we continue to shy away from in the Church. It is also something to which Jesus appears to explicitly refer in St Matthew's Gospel (5:27-28).

Some commentators who are opposed to sexual lives for LGBTQI people will recognise the short-sightedness of a position that attempts to categorise acts, and instead will suggest that sexual acts are 'what you wouldn't do with a friend'. Taking the most generous interpretation of this statement, we might see within it a recognition that it is both meaning and act that work together to define that which is sexual – and therefore, that which is forbidden to

LGBTQI people. However, it is by taking a step back and considering what this prohibition means that we recognise the utter inhumanity of such a position. To accept that acts and meaning are required to define sexual life is to situate sexual activity in relationship between two people – whether that is a relationship of romantic love or, as has become more common particularly in the 'App generation', simply a relationship of short-term mutual desire (a position that we will return to in Part III of this book).

The traditional Christian view has been that the former of these kinds of relationship is the proper place for sexual expression – a position that across the centuries has led to the defining of marriage as the ultimate (and, more recently, only) place for such expression. Yet for those who oppose LGBTQI sexual lives, it appears that their reading of the Bible is that such relationships – not just sex – should be denied to people of the same sex. Of course, not all such relationships include 'genital acts', either at the present moment or even at all, yet we are able to describe such relationships, however intangibly, as fundamentally different in nature to that between friends. It appears intellectually incoherent to try to define only some behaviour in these relationships as sexual. We are learning that human beings are coherent, integrated wholes, in which the being and acting work together in relationship. A prohibition on sex is a prohibition on sexual relationship, with or without genital acts. This is the problem with a focus on acts and prohibition, rather than on interior disposition – it leads to intellectual catastrophe. It ultimately highlights how it is often an ideology – or at the very least, a particular way of understanding the human person – that precedes biblical interpretations that lead to the side-lining of the LGBTQI person in this way.

None of this, of course, is an argument for a free-for-all, however much those who oppose LGBTQI sexual relationships might create that particular straw man. The key argument of this book is the importance of holding up biblical insights against insights from human knowledge – not a rejection of the Bible. If, as Christians, we believe that there is no such thing as the secular and sacred, but rather an integrated whole under the Lordship of Christ, then it is a false dichotomy to pit one against the other. Instead, it is far more coherent to see the two as complementary, the Bible guiding our interpretation of human knowledge, and human knowledge contributing to our ability to understand the insights of the Bible in each new age.

As we shall see in later chapters, the Bible, together with Christian tradition and history, does have much to say about the right ordering of relationship, focused not on sexual acts but primarily on the relationship that those acts point to. It is for this reason that committed monogamous sexual relationships have been lauded by the Church, and why some forms of relationship – amongst them abusive, predatory, paedophilic or destructive – have been utterly opposed. It is not simply the acts in these relationships which are the issue – repugnant and dehumanising as they often are – but the relationship to which these acts point. These kinds of relationship do not include the essential factors of human love – amongst them consent and free choice. Because of this, such relationships can never be humanising or fulfilling, and nor can they ever lead to human flourishing, because the core is rotten. Those who carry these kinds of desire must, then, not act on them, because doing so would reduce, rather than increase, their own humanity.

Thus, it is not always right to act on innate desires, even if those desires form part of one's psychological make-up, and hence not only one's sense of self but even one's actual self. To recommend, and even demand, abstinence from action is a significant thing, because the repression of the self carries with it significant psychological baggage, and may well lead to harm in and of itself. Thus, for those who must not act, by virtue of their acted-out desires potentially leading to abusive and dehumanising relationship, it is essential that the right support and underlying psychological analysis is provided.

It may be easier to ignore for those people who do not have such desires, but the psyche of these people may be extremely damaged, often through abuse they themselves have suffered. It is a simple solution to criminalise and demonise those who are unable to form healthy relationships; instead, and most particularly as a church, we should be much more willing to see this as a psychological issue that might indeed respond to treatment and may require a great deal more compassion than we currently offer.

That is not for one moment to excuse the behaviour of those who act and cause untold harm to vulnerable adults and children. Abuse in all its forms is an abhorrent crime that strikes at the very heart of the humanity of the other, and for far too long has not been taken seriously enough by a church desperate to protect its own reputation. We must, however, be open to the possibility that our unwillingness to talk about healthy, or unhealthy, relationships or be willing to offer genuine support and therapeutic engagement to such people before any such acts occur is unwittingly making a successful, safe and appropriate outcome even harder. Those who abuse others in unhealthy relationships should most certainly face the consequences; yet we who do nothing to identify and address the deeply problematical psychological damage and instead solely focus on criminal justice may simply be making the problem worse.

This brief foray into genuinely unhealthy relationships leads us back to the arguments made by those who are opposed to same-sex relationships that include all such relationships in this 'forbidden' category. Whilst at last many opponents of same-sex relationships seem to have recognised that there is nothing intrinsically abusive about same-sex relationships, nonetheless the argument is made that these relationships are against the will of God and thus must not be entered into. The only option, then, is to reject any possibility of a sexual, fulfilled human relationship with someone of the same sex, and instead to repress one's feelings, desires, and innate personality. As we have described, to do so poses huge risks. Repression carries with it enormously damaging psychological consequences, which will often pose huge risks to an individual's mental and physical health.

Repression is one of a number of different defence mechanisms identified by psychologists.[5] These are often separated into those which are pathological, immature, neurotic and mature – each likely to lead to a particular state of mind and ultimately physical health. At the damaging end, these move from denial and delusion, to passive-aggression, projection and fantasy, through displacement, dissociation and repression. Some of these mechanisms may indeed have short-term benefits – allowing individuals to cope with the world around them and reduce the stress and anxiety caused by the world. For some LGBTQI Christians, adopting these kinds of mechanisms may well help them to cope with the internal cognitive dissonance they feel, where their identity is facing constant onslaught from those demanding they take leave of part of their self – indeed, their identity conflict may in fact result entirely from internalisation of external, destructive criticism. Yet such defence mechanisms are poor substitutes for true coping strategies – instead, they lead to long-term relationship difficulties, and often lead to individuals who are horribly caught up in what is eventually tantamount to emotional self-abuse. It is these kind of defence mechanisms that therapy aims to address – yet these are the very strategies that Christians appear to wish to force upon their LGBTQI siblings in Christ.

At the other end of the defence mechanism ladder are those strategies commonly referred to as 'mature'. These include altruism, humour, sublimation and suppression

---

[5] The general psychological reading recommended above may be useful here too. In addition, readers may be interested in Morvan, C., and O'Connor, A., *An Analysis of Leon Festinger's A Theory of Cognitive Dissonance* (London: Macat, 2017) and Hentschel, U., et al, eds., *The Concept of Defence Mechanisms in Contemporary Psychology* (New York: Springer, 1993).

– the last being a conscious decision to delay attention paid to something for a particular period in time, yet with the recognition that it will need to be addressed at a later date (quite different to repression, in which the individual unconsciously blocks desires that they find, or have been told are, unacceptable). For those who argue same-sex relationships are unacceptable, it may be that these defence mechanisms appear to offer the psychological key. However, the mature mechanisms require us to have a healthy and conscious relationship with reality. This brings us back to the integrated whole we referred to earlier in this chapter – it is a nonsense to expect a healthy and conscious relationship with reality to reject the facet of the self that is sexuality. It is, ultimately, a logical fallacy – and is amongst the multitude of reasons that any attempt at 'conversion therapy' is so opposed by any serious psychological professional.

Conversion therapy – the ultimate form of repression and denial – is known to lead to serious adverse mental health consequences, and it is now incontrovertible that sexuality cannot be changed through this kind of psychological torture. The ex-gay movement is so thoroughly discredited as to make discussion of it in these pages unnecessary, yet it is important to note that much of this movement is not that far away from those who continue to believe in the use of prayer to repress, if not change, sexuality. Whilst changing from gay to straight appears more dramatic, the belief that praying hard enough will change individuals from those with sexual desires to those who don't is just as absurd. We return back to the difficulty we keep finding in this chapter – that sexuality and relationship are far too closely (even inextricably) linked, and to try to force them apart is entirely contrary to human flourishing, whether an explicitly Christian account or otherwise.

All that being said, it is important to be clear that human lives can be entirely fulfilled without sex. Nothing that has been said so far is to cast aspersions on those who live without a sexual element in their lives – whether lifelong or at particular life stages. Such people fall into a number of categories – some choose to be abstinent and some are forced into it through circumstance beyond their control. For some people, 'genital acts' will be physically impossible, although with the more generous interpretation of sexual lives as advocated in this chapter, it is not entirely clear that they do not live sexually, if not in the same manifestation as others. There is a rich Christian history of celibacy – which can be both healthy and life-giving, most particularly when freely chosen. Recent years have shown some of the dangers of enforced celibacy in clergy of the Roman Catholic Church – once again, this is not an argument to excuse the sickening abuse scandals, but rather to offer at least one possible line of explanation for where ordinary human desires became disordered and led to such despicable acts against children and other vulnerable people.

One of the key differences between voluntary and enforced celibacy is how it might fit into the defence mechanisms discussed above. Of course, for some people, there is no sexual drive and there is thus no particular impulse to engage and work with in the case of celibacy. It is outside the scope of this book to fully consider asexuality, but nonetheless it is clear that such people live fulfilled lives that engage relationships in a whole variety of different ways and yet in ways that can prove intensely beneficial to these individuals and to society more generally. For those, however, who do choose celibacy despite having a sexual drive, such a decision must be made with eyes open to the possible negative outcomes of any such self-denial. This kind of serious commitment opens the possibility of the mature mechanisms mentioned, and as a free choice is something that individuals have the opportunity to commit to and offer to God or their fellow humanity in a way that can be healthy and life-giving.

The problem comes when celibacy is enforced – and an example of this would be the barrage of pro-celibacy arguments that are launched at LGBTQI people. This is not a free choice, and because of this the commitments made and the internal psychological perspective are fundamentally different. Celibacy – or rather enforced abstinence – is no longer a gift freely received but becomes an external demand that carries with it several levels of incoherence. It is not possible to freely choose abstinence when the 'alternative' offered is not only eternal damnation but also rejection by friends and family, the Church more widely and often entire support networks. We then enter into territory that demands sacrifice and suffering for its own sake (or allegedly in pursuit of a higher 'godly' goal) – often justified by a selective appeal to scripture, a recognition of the bind in which this puts LGBTQI people, and a tacit acceptance that God has made LGBTQI people (and them only) a particular way in order that they might somehow share in his suffering, an idea returned to later in this book.[6]

It is particularly easy, of course, for straight people to demand something of LGBTQI people when they have no experience of the psychological effects of coming out – which can often be traumatic – let alone will never be faced with such a demand to deny oneself. It is easy for those who can go back to their wives or husbands to call such a self-denial as the 'taking up of the cross' for LGBTQI people. It is extraordinary that so many straight people do not recognise the lack of introspection they show when they describe these demands in the abstract. It is unfailingly cruel to demand something of LGBTQI people without even a thought as to how that might affect them, particularly when you live in a

---

[6] A version of this argument is found in Shaw, E., *The Plausibility Problem* (London: Inter-Varsity, 2015) and further developed in Shaw, E., *Purposeful Sexuality* (London: Inter-Varsity, 2021). This is an unusual example of someone who is himself gay, and yet holds to a view of Christianity that forbids any sexual expression because of this fact. Shaw appears to recognise that the version of God he describes poses serious questions for LGBTQI people but is unable to reconcile this with his own experience of sexuality without making use (at least in part) of such an argument. It is hard to see how a healthy sexual ethic can possibly be derived from these two books.

world in which your own right to self-expression has never and will never be questioned. Those who we met in the first chapter, who talk about the Church needing time to adapt, however personally supportive they are, need to look at this square in the face. Bishops who call for further discussion are often the very bishops who will then go home to their wives at home, and not see the glaring inadequacy of their response or the hypocrisy embedded in these kinds of call for more time.

5

LIFE IN ALL ITS FULLNESS
PART II

It is probably useful, at this point, to outline the three broad ways that scientific progress is generally made, not least because church leaders so often – either deliberately or accidentally – mix them up or elide them into one another. The first kind of scientific progress is discovery about the world. Discovery might include understanding the finer points of the immune system, or about plate tectonics, or about our genetic make-up. It is empirical, in the main – it is testable, and a true discovery ends up with so much evidence stacked in its favour as to make it extraordinarily unlikely that an alternative is correct. All science is, of course, open to challenge, yet for some discoveries, the evidence is so strong that we can truly say we have learnt something new about the world. Sometimes these discoveries can come out of the blue – the testing of a meteorite to better understand its physical make-up, for example – and will often rely on the third broad method of discovery outlined below. Sometimes, this type of discovery can come out of simple observation, that is aligned with a theory, which helps us to predict what is likely in other, similar, circumstances.

Secondly, and closely related to the first, are discoveries that remain primarily theoretical, whether because the evidence is not yet quite convincing enough to declare something extremely likely, or because the workings out will always remain theoretical (an example of which might be elements of theoretical physics). Scientists often use something called the 'p value', which in short is a measure of how unlikely it would be to find the results you do purely by chance. In fact, scientists start with the null hypothesis – that there is no difference, for example, between two samples you are looking at – and then work from there, to convince themselves, and their peers, that what they believe they are seeing really does hit statistical significance. Experiments help us develop a better and better understanding as to whether the explanation we have found is convincing, or whether an alternative needs to be sought. Good science is that which opens itself up to testing by others, and which relies not only on peer review but on the possibility of being overturned if the evidence points in a different direction. Theories are, however, contingent – good scientists do not see their theories as immutable, but as entirely open to change as the evidence suggests. That said, even in the scientific community, some might occasionally declare something as being in the first category here where it should be in the second.

The third type of discovery is that which relates to technology. This is included because it is so often used as a scare tactic by religious leaders who want to besmirch science. The development of a scientific technique is generally utilising some underlying theory to enable a manipulation of some physical entity – whether inert or living – to make some kind of change to the way it is working, or to enable us to test something we otherwise wouldn't be able to. Key examples might be the ability to test molecules in the blood, or measure seismic waves, or the ability to send satellites into space. Very often this kind of discovery is met with what purports to be a 'conservative' view-point from those in religious leadership – that more testing is needed, or that such a technique might be unnatural. In recent years, this kind of fear of the unknown has grown in pace – we need look only to the recent development of mitochondrial transfer therapy, or pre-implantation genetic diagnosis, to see how easy it is to label the technique, rather than potential forms of its implementation, as intrinsically bad.

Some of this fear doubtless comes from a worrying lack of scientific literacy amongst religious leaders – and sadly, amongst the general public more widely. As humans, we often fear those things that we do not fully understand, and our fear can even prevent us investigating them further. Yet that is not to say that some fear – or at least conservatism – is not in order on occasion. We need only look back at the last century to see how the wonders of modern technology can be used to inflict terror and suffering, whether in the development of the atom bomb, or in the inhumane experiments of the Nazi death camps. Yet religious leaders often make one of two mistakes, which renders their criticism and genuine concern significantly less effective.

The first of these is to focus on the wrong thing. To take the atom bomb as an example, it is surely one of the greatest indictments of humankind that one of the key technological discoveries of recent times has been used to create a bomb that could ultimately destroy humanity. Yet the very same technology may soon become the key to solving our seemingly never-ending obsession with and demand for fossil fuels. Similarly the technology, called Crispr-Cas9, used a few years ago to huge outcry, to modify foetal DNA to produce babies that would be 'immune' to HIV (yet with as yet unknown side effects or long term sequelae) may hold the answer to treating and possibly even curing other debilitating and horrendous diseases. The technology is not the issue – it is how it is used. Religious leaders need to focus more on this act of curating, and focus their concern on the 'how' rather than the 'what'. The acquisition of human knowledge is not the problem – it is how this is done, and how it is used that is the key.[1]

---

[1] A discussion of these themes can be found in Massmann, A., and Fox, K. R., *Modifying Our Genes: Theology, Science and 'Playing God'* (London: SCM Press, 2021).

The other way that religious leaders get it so badly wrong in their interventions on technological advance is to conflate technology – and primarily its use – with all of science, as though the use of genetic modification is the same as the discovery of subatomic particles. This hermeneutic of suspicion towards all of science is highly damaging to the prospects of religion being taken seriously on its own terms and being taken seriously as an agent of dialogue with science. There is much in the history of how scientific discoveries were made that is not morally neutral; likewise, there is much in the future of how these discoveries will be put to use that is not morally neutral either. Yet until the Church is able to get beyond generalised suspicion, its often-knee-jerk reactions and outright hostility to science remain a significant stumbling block to any positive influence it might have.

It is worth briefly considering the role of the social sciences, which includes to some degree elements of psychology – particularly that outside experimental psychology. Theories in social sciences share a lot in common with the natural sciences – they are an attempt to make sense out of human and societal interactions, and to develop frameworks and models that best explain what is happening and point to possible future interventions. These are often tested in ways that may not offer such a stable statistical basis as that found in the natural sciences – in part because of huge numbers of confounding factors and because human populations are so varied and influenced by their culture. It is certainly true that different schools of thought exist across the social sciences, and two different theories may use entirely different methods to explain observed human phenomena. Yet at their heart, social and psychological theories are aiming to produce frameworks that are effective, reproducible, predictive and help explain the way that human beings act by observing and by recognising the key importance of culture and context. They may contain biases and presuppositions – but as more and more evidence is found, and as they are tested and rigorously examined, certain key features become more and more pronounced. It is through this kind of process that overwhelming evidence develops. To reject it outright, and the science that supports it, is nothing short of scandalous.

In all the forms of scientific enquiry that we have outlined, a key facet has been that of the phenomenon – that which is observed to exist. It is through the description of, and an attempt to find explanation for, phenomena that the scientific method has radically changed humanity in the last few centuries. Unfortunately, it seems that the Church has not yet recognised the key change this has brought about in society, or the enormous possibilities that this opens up for the Church itself. The phenomenon of homosexuality, for example, can be viewed from a number of different perspectives – the genetic, the environmental, the zoological, the anthropological, the psychological and the sociological. All of these together point to a number of very clear positions:

- that sexual variation is normal, and that there are clear exceptions to the XY binary genetics;[2]
- that homosexual activity is found throughout nature;[3]
- that in humans, homosexuality forms part of a variation in sexual lives and that sexual orientation is not a choice but an innate part of the mature human personality, with some genetic and some developmental environmental factors involved (as in almost all human traits);[4]

[2] A good review is found in Ainsworth, C., 'Sex redefined', *Nature* (2015) 518:288-291.
[3] A discussion can be found in Sommer, V., and Vasey, P. L., eds., *Behaviour in Animals: An Evolutionary Perspective* (Cambridge: Cambridge University Press, 2006).
[4] Readers may wish to read further in this area. A starting point might be Balthazart, J., *The Biology of Homosexuality* (Oxford: Oxford University Press, 2011) or Wilson, G., and Rahman, Q., *Born Gay: the Psychobiology of Sex Orientation* (London: Peter Owen, 2008). There are also a number of primary genetic studies – amongst the most recent is Ganna, A., et al., 'Large-scale GWAS reveals insights into the genetic architecture of same-sex sexual behavior', *Science* (2019) 365 (6456). Once again, some theological writers have picked and chosen particular studies to fit their agendas, but it is essential that we commit ourselves to a serious interrogation of what is known if we are to make judgements about its implications.

- that sexual orientation cannot be changed through the volition of the individual concerned;[5]
- that great psychological damage can be done to LGBTQI people if attempts are made to split apart their identity;[6]
- that LGBTQI people can and do live lives which are equivalent in terms of many different measures of human flourishing to those who are straight;[7]
- that the greatest challenge to LGBTQI flourishing is prejudice from without.[8]

These are not ideological propositions – they are factual statements supported by the overwhelming evidence from these different fields and are the canvas with which any discussion of LGBTQI people must start. Those who argue that a 'biblical' view contrasts with these facts needs to recognise that we are comparing apples and oranges – these are not a 'perspective' but the ever-strengthening knowledge base that we have from observation and the scientific method. This is the phenomenon of homosexuality; it is upon that phenomenon that any ideology or theology must build and to which it must be applied. The holy scriptures may indeed contain all things necessary to our salvation, and be the revelation of God Himself, but God also created the heavens and the Earth, including the intellect and rationality of human beings. It is inconceivable that He could want us to ignore observed phenomena when reading and interpreting the Bible.

---

[5] Further to this, the concept of 'conversion therapy' has been opposed by all major psychiatric, paediatric and psychological bodies in the UK. Further discussion of the ineffectiveness and damage caused by 'conversion therapy' is found in Haldeman, D. C. (ed.), *The Case Against Conversion 'Therapy': Evidence, Ethics, and Alternatives* (Washington DC: APA, 2021).

[6] See footnote above.

[7] Interested readers may enjoy Todd, M., *Straight Jacket* (London: Penguin, 2018) which addresses flourishing in LBGTQI people, and some of the malevolent forces that prevent or oppose it.

[8] See footnote above.

It is worth briefly addressing the genetic basis of human sex, if only to show the importance of sensitive and careful application of scripture to observed phenomena. Human beings have two sets of chromosomes, one inherited from each biological parent, making a total of forty-six in all. Two of these chromosomes are the key to whether an individual is described as male or female at birth – and in the main these form a combination of either XX or XY. Females have two X chromosomes, and males have XY – once again, in most cases. The other chromosomes play no part in sexual differentiation, although a process called imprinting (a discussion of which is outside the scope of this book) does mean that some gene expression is different depending on whether particular chromosomes have come from a male or female biological parent. Ultimately, the role of DNA is to code for proteins that make up a cell, and alongside these genes there are regulatory regions on the DNA and regulatory molecules that allow different proteins to be expressed in different cells. It's ultimately down to this differential expression that our liver cells, for example, look and behave differently to our neurones.

That said, it's the 'most cases' which is interesting here, because there are exceptions. Before delving into those, it's worth highlighting what we might mean by 'biological sex'. It's probably easiest to see this as divided into three different categories. Firstly, we have genetic sex – as we have described above – based on the specific chromosomal combination that has been inherited from mother and father. Secondly, we have gonadal sex – in essence, a description of whatever sexual organs have developed (either testes or ovary, generally with their associated gametes). Thirdly, we have what might be described as somatic sex – that describes those sexual characteristics that we classically associate with male or female, both the secondary sex organs such as the penis, vagina and uterus, and those characteristics which develop more in puberty, such as body hair, breast development, and similar. Each of these categories of sexual differentiation interact with each other – the genes ultimately produce proteins which lead to hormonal changes, which feedback on gene expression and cellular differentiation. Such a complex network provides a fertile ground for biological variation to occur.

Above, we have noted that XY almost always produces males. However, what is really key to this differentiation is a tiny region on an already tiny chromosome, called the *sry* region. This region encodes something called a transcription factor – an area of DNA that will ultimately control the production of protein from other parts of the DNA. If this *sry* region is missing, then you will end up with a genetic, gonadal and somatic female, whether the remainder of that chromosome is Y or otherwise. Likewise, if you end up with cells that happen to be unresponsive to testosterone or other sex hormones, you can end up with individuals in whom the genetic, gonadal and somatic sex differentiation does not neatly match up. For some, sexual differentiation leads to a set of intersex characteristics – either primary hermaphroditism, in which individuals have both ovarian and testicular tissue, or secondary hermaphroditism, in which there may be ambiguity of external sexual organs or an observed somatic picture that does not easily fit into either simply male or female.

It turns out that human sexual differentiation is not quite as simple as we might have thought. This is the reality of human life, and it is to this phenomenon that the Bible must be able to speak – this is indeed a challenge to the narrative of gender complementarity or even to the essential nature of gender in creation, but it is a challenge that is born out of the reality of human existence. The answer surely cannot be to ignore intersex people, or to demand that because it's out of the ordinary, they must remain abstinent from sexual relationship. One poor argument that has been advanced, that this lack of effective sexual differentiation is a result of the Fall (and is thus not God's will for creation) does not hold water when we recognise that the processes that lead to intersex characteristics are inevitable in a genetic and hormonal biological system. Once again, we cannot attempt to do theology that ignores the reality of the world that God has given us. Regression to the Fall is not good theology. The reality is that human experience and knowledge can improve, rather than tear down, our interpretation of scripture – and it does not threaten the primacy of scripture. Yet to ignore it means reading scripture through a lens that is ultimately untrue, and no number of appeals to the male and female in the Eden myth will allow us to avoid this simple fact. This is the issue for those who find simple binaries in the Bible – it doesn't reflect the world God created. Our knowledge of the world, instead, calls us to revisit and discern what is truly at the heart of these stories of relationship.

A final element of biology that is worth spelling out is the ever-circling debate in church circles, but not in scientific ones, about the existence of the 'gay gene'. To be blunt, there is no evidence whatsoever that such a gene exists. The great majority of human traits are influenced by our genetics, by the uterine environment, by our biological parents' biology, by our upbringing – sociological, psychological and biological factors all playing a part – and by our maturing as adults. That homosexuality would be a special case speaks more to ignorance than to serious scientific endeavour. As we move through life, our cellular differentiation becomes fixed, and as we know from many other character and personality traits, this process of biological maturing doubtless leads to our psychological and neurological networks becoming more concrete. Whilst we may be able to fine tune ourselves psychologically, in no other key psychological characteristic is there any evidence of change occurring. It is shocking that the Church continues to treat sexuality as if all the insights of modern science and medicine have nothing to say about it.

Knowing what we do about the phenomenon of human sexuality, we are right now to ask what human flourishing might look like. This, of course, is a challenging area, although there are certainly some commonalities that come to us from both scripture and human knowledge. From a psychological perspective, Maslow's hierarchy of human needs is a good place to start, as it separates out 'deficiency' needs from 'growth' needs. Whilst there remains some controversy about the order of needs in his famous pyramid, nonetheless the stages are indicative of what we might look for in measures of human flourishing. These include, as 'deficiency' needs, physiological, safety, social belonging and love, and esteem, and as 'growth' needs, include cognitive, aesthetic, self-actualisation and transcendence. From all that we have looked at in this section of the book, it is clear that a healthy and fulfilling sexuality permeates throughout each of these needs, and similarly that there is no intrinsic reason that LGBTQI people should have any differing needs to straight people. Secular work on human flourishing increasingly looks at the whole person – both as an entire individual and as someone in relationship, in community. It is not enough to point to specific elements – each element forms part of an interconnected whole.

It is interesting to note that the historical tradition of Christianity leads to similar understandings of what human flourishing might look for. That great Christian martyr of the second century AD, Irenaeus, wrote of 'vivens homo' in his oft misquoted work *Against Heresies*, and many a time the surrounding passage has been translated as 'the glory of God is a human being fully alive'. Alas, whilst this works beautifully for procuring a sound bite, it misses the remainder of the passage – in which Irenaeus makes it clear that it is in Christ that we see what being fully alive looks like. 'The life of humankind comes from the vision of God', he tells us, and it is in Christ Himself that we see true human flourishing. It is not a Christ who married – who, indeed, appears to have chosen the way of celibacy – or whose witness points towards psychological damage in the form of coercive denial of loving relationship. This is the same Christ whose life points towards loving relationship, as we saw in Chapter 2, and who looked into the heart of those he met as integrated wholes. Christ's way is one that doesn't pigeon-hole or seek to create separate parts of the self, but rather recognises their interconnectedness and the essential nature of this to the formation of the Christian. As St Maximus the Confessor stated:

> The mystery of the incarnation of the *Logos* holds the power of all the hidden meanings (*logoi*) and figures of Scripture as well as the knowledge of visible and intelligible creatures. Whoever knows the mystery of the cross and the tomb knows the principles (*logoi*) of these creatures, and whoever has been initiated into the ineffable power of the resurrection knows the purpose (*logos*) for which God originally made all things.[9]

We each bring our own sociocultural baggage to the table on questions of human flourishing, and it is of course arguable that much of human knowledge is tinged with this as well. Our opinions on homosexuality are also culturally mediated – for thousands of years LGBTQI people have been marginalised, and those steeped in the Church cannot help but have imbibed a little of this implicit homophobia. Meanwhile, the world has been faced with and struggled with the question of LGBTQI inclusion in an often fractious, but far more open manner. We hear much about standing up to the values of the world, as though the Church is somehow performing a martyr's role in opposing same-sex relationships. This does appear to ignore the vast history of homophobia, particularly in the west, and those who truly believe their biblical interpretation is not affected by their own sociocultural baggage are either mistaken or wilfully ignorant. In many ways, it is extraordinary that so many within the Church have managed to throw off this baggage, of so many different ages.

Yet we will not be able to throw off our cultural baggage

---

[9] Quoted and translated by Beeley, C.A., 'Christ and Human Flourishing in Patristic Theology', *Pro Ecclesia: A Journal of Catholic and Evangelical Theology* (2016) 25 (2): 126-153. Readers may enjoy the entire article for further discussion of patristic notions of human flourishing.

if we do not use all of the tools we have at our disposal to do so. Returning to the theme of Chapter 2 and 3, we have been gifted the three-legged stool of Scripture, Tradition and Reason, and if we are to seriously engage in these questions of human flourishing, we need to make the most of it – indeed, it is an Anglican gift to the wider church. Our theological propositions must be tried and tested by their ability to inform and contribute to wider understandings of human flourishing. Indeed, our propositional theology must move to one of such tripartite dialogue. The secular literature on human flourishing continues to grow, and our own Christian tradition is full of insights, explicitly scriptural and otherwise. It is to human flourishing that we must return if we are to understand the place of LGBTQI people in the Church and the world – a view that asks not what goes where but what the heart is doing in the presence of God. If - as we have seen briefly in this chapter, and will consider in the next section, and see time and again in the secular literature - the evidence on flourishing goes against our own inherited position on LGBTQI people, then we need to rely on more than proof texting if we are to argue for a continuation of the current non-affirming position.

There is also significant precedent for the taking of experience and reason seriously. For many centuries, and most particularly in the work of St Thomas Aquinas, natural theology has been used to attempt to understand God through observation of the world. Whilst the teleological argument – the argument from intelligent design – has well and truly run its course, there is no good reason to throw out the natural world as a place where theology can be done. Arguments around what is 'natural' and what is not ultimately appears to be bound to fail – we have seen this with discussions around homosexuality and arguments around the natural or proper place for genitalia to fulfil their function. The argument that because the penis fits within the vagina then all sex should be heterosexual penetrative is not a strong one, although it does remain central to the argument of some opponents of

LBGTQI sexuality.[10] To try to guess the mind of God from any humanly identified 'proper way of things' in terms of particular functions or particular body parts is once again falling into the 'acts' trap. But if we turn to our study of nature and investigate and interrogate the systems and networks that make up communities, relationships and individuals, then it is foolhardy indeed to reject what the scientific method has given us. Indeed, any contemporary appeal to natural law must make a serious attempt to understand what the natural world actually is.

For catholic Christians, indeed – amongst whom is counted the Church of England – God is revealed not only in word but also in sacrament – both pointing to the Word, Jesus Christ. Experience, then, is a matter of fundamental importance to Christians because of the very way that God makes Himself known within the Church. Therefore, whilst our prime argument has been an encouragement to take rigorous, evidenced academic work seriously as a gift from God, we should nonetheless not reject the narratives of individual Christians. If we look at the lives of Christian LGBTQI people who live faithfully, lovingly, in sexually active relationships, can we really turn to them and say that their lives portray sin and destruction any more than straight couples do? It is very hard indeed to look at the huge number of examples of faithful, long-standing commitment both to the other and to the Church, and to call this all evil – an aberration, despised of God. You cannot love the sinner but hate the sin, when the 'sin' is a key part of what

[10]   A particular example of this is found in Gagnon, R. A. J., *The Bible and Homosexual Practice* (Nashville: Abingdon, 2001). Gagnon argues that because a penis and vagina complement each other, then heterosexuality is normative and thus natural. This argument – and several others posited in Gagnon's account – are carefully decimated in David Atkinson, 'The Church of England and Homosexuality' in Brown, T. (ed.), *Other Voices, Other Worlds: Global Church Speaks out on Homosexuality* (London: Darton, Longman and Todd, 2006). Atkinson correctly states that Gagnon's book is 'an exhaustive exegetical study, but unfortunately proclaims a certainty which I do not believe his argument supports' (p. 307). Brown's text is worth consulting for further discussion of the contextual nature of much church-based conversation on homosexuality.

builds up these beautiful relationships of overflowing love. Do we really dare to call what God appears to have blessed in its fruits evil?

The Bible, in one sense, does have all the answers – the problem is that one of the Bible's own answers is to take narrative and human knowledge seriously. The argument that homosexuality is wrong because of spurious claims that contradict the entirety of human experience and knowledge, feels like the slow dying of an old order that has gone astray from serious, biblical, Christian theology. The argument fails not only because it causes real hurt to real LGBTQI people, but because it flies in the face of the notion of human flourishing found deep in the heart of biblical, Christian theology.

Human dignity is at the heart of human flourishing, as is the promotion of a human integrity that incorporates and respects the physical, social, psychological and spiritual. The Bible tells us so; the human sciences tell us so. The experience of godly LGTBQI people living lives in love and faith tells us so.

Let anyone who has an ear listen to what the Spirit is saying to the churches.

(Revelation 2:29)

PART II

6

EXPRESSION OR
REPRESSION

In the first part of this book, we have laid out the central thesis – that it is not only irrational but goes strongly against the grain of the entire tenor of Christian history, tradition and scripture to ignore both discovery and experience. We have begun to sketch out what a theology that took human knowledge seriously might look like, and seen that the insights from the knowledge have a lot to offer, complement and dialogue with Christian narratives of human flourishing. In this Section, we move towards looking at the good and the bad in the current church discussions on this topic – and in the lives of LGBTQI people who are too often the target of others' opinions, and too little recognised as the beloved people of God that they are.

We will consider contrasting alternatives of how the Church might behave and interrogate what this dialogue of narratives might tell us about what God is doing. We will hear stories of faithful Christians in whose lives the Spirit of God is clear to see, and we will hear stories of what terrible damage can be done when we turn away from inclusion, expression and openness towards exclusion, repression and erasure. We will ask, with our eyes wide open, what God appears to be doing and what the effect of getting this wrong might be on the mission and ministry of the Church that he has entrusted to us.

In this chapter, we will think particularly about the effect of repression on the psychology and personal identity of LGBTQI people. We will see examples of where things have gone right and where things have gone wrong, and ask where God seems to be amidst the different approaches. We know that an individual's behaviour can not only lead to particular outcomes (negative or positive) in and of themselves but also can innately shape that individual's personality – not only from psychological studies but from theological narratives of human flourishing, in which the whole rather than the parts must always be considered. We will look, then, at the violence that is done by repression not only to the victims of others' behaviour, but to the individual themselves. Finally, we will ask: is this kind of damage really what the Lord is asking for in the lives of LGBTQI people?

It is worth defining what we mean by repression. Repression can take a number of forms – it can include the conscious or the subconscious exclusion of desire or other thoughts and feelings from the conscious mind, and also a refusal to talk and be open about these desires, thoughts and feelings. It can be internally or externally imposed and can indeed result from a mixture of the two. It is not always a negative process – or perhaps more properly, it is not always inappropriate to wish to remove some thoughts, feelings and desires, although as we saw in Chapters 4 and 5 the psychological process of 'repression' is not a generally healthy one. Yet repression – either as an atmosphere or as a specific process in any one individual – that is not acknowledged or properly processed can lead to significant mental distress, however laudable the aim of the repression itself, and very infrequently leads to anything like a good outcome in terms of the long-term flourishing of either the individual or community more widely.

Repression, of course, has been one of humanity's key dialogue partners in the conversation (or rather, lack of conversation) about and with homosexuality. For centuries, and most particularly seen in recent centuries in the western world, homosexuality was the 'love that dare not speak its name'.[1] Homosexual activity was frequently punished by long prison sentences, if not death, and the kind of contemporary conversations around sexual desire – let alone expression – would have been unthinkable even a century ago. There are still parts of the world where any 'homosexual activity' can lead to execution – shamefully, these penal systems are almost without exception those based on theocratic legal theory.[2] What is just as shocking is that – despite calls from the Anglican Communion – there are still churches and bishops that claim the name Anglican who are either covertly or – in some cases – overtly encouraging extremely strict criminal action against 'practising homosexuals'.[3] This is, certainly, extreme – yet these are the same churches and prelates that many argue should be listened to and made concessions to when other churches within the Anglican Communion discuss homosexuality.

It is beyond the scope of this book to discuss in depth the cultural reasons why some provinces of the Anglican Communion continue to express revulsion about homosexuality, but it is doubtless an issue of sociocultural – which may include religious and colonialist – conditioning.[4] The impressive and detailed work of Martha Nussbaum on

[1] The full poem – 'Two Loves', by Alfred Lord Douglas – is well worth reading in light of the discussions in this section of the book and reflecting on the current cultural context that still exists in the Church.
[2] Amnesty International is a key body that identifies and calls out these continued judicial outrages.
[3] A recent situation arose in Ghana in late 2021, in which an 'Anti-LGBTQ bill' was proposed by opposition parties and actively sponsored by churches, amongst them the Anglican Church in Ghana – amongst the proposed Bill's provisions was imprisonment for LGBTQI people and their supporters, forced medical procedures on intersex people, and 'conversion therapy'. Whilst slow in coming, there was eventually stated (albeit qualified) opposition against this Bill from the Church of England, and a reminder to Anglican primates that they had all agreed to work against homophobia in a communique released in 2016.
[4] The previously mentioned *Other Voices, Other Worlds* is an introduction to this area particularly from a religious point of view, although in the secular sphere much has also been written.

the philosophy of disgust bears great attention,[5] and it is doubtless an underlying concept of heteronormative disgust coupled with societal 'propriety' norms that continues to lead to the horrific abuse of LGBTQI people in these settings, and the exporting of this kind of prejudice into wider church discussions. That is not, of course, to say that it is only in certain geographical locations – often in the majority or developing world – that such prejudice exists, but it is rather a comment on the link between the openness of society to discussions on this topic and the kind of social and political commentary and ultimately penal systems that exist in any such society. Such openness – or lack of – can be seen at a national, regional or local level, and we are far too good at pointing out the speck in the eye of other churches than at noticing the huge planks that remain in many of our own communities. It is shameful that conversations about LGBTQI people remain controversial in our churches in this day and age, with some churches refusing to engage in the recent Living in Love and Faith initiative because the conversations within congregations were too difficult or delicate.[6] This is not a healthy faith, and we need to sort our own problems out before pointing fingers at the rest of the world. Not offending other churches in the communion has become far too convenient a scapegoat for our own lack of action.

Unfortunately, many parts of the majority world – most particularly those in Africa – have been used as pawns in a global fight by many American fundamentalist evangelicals who are obsessed with homosexuality, and who utilise their

---

[5] A good starting point would be Nussbaum, M. C., *From Disgust to Humanity: Sexual Orientation and Constitutional Law* (Oxford: Oxford University Press, 2010).

[6] *Living in Love and Faith* is the most recent initiative in a long line of initiatives run by the Church of England, to continue the 'conversation' about LGBTQI issues. It arose out of the rejection, by the clergy members of the governing body of the Church of England (General Synod), of a statement from the bishops that essentially made no change in church doctrine or policy following a period of listening. More can be found about *Living in Love and Faith* on the Church of England's website (https://www.churchofengland.org/resources/living-love-and-faith).

money in ways as to secure the most influence in this game.[7] To them, such people are entirely expendable but useful pawns in a proxy war, and money is given with strings attached to secure the most vicious and prejudicial anti-LGBTQI laws and attitudes that money can buy. Yet it is far too easy to forget the LGBTQI people who live in such places and who directly suffer as a result of this hatred and prejudice. It is patent nonsense when some African leaders state that homosexuality is 'un-African', as sociologists, historians and theologians have shown,[8] yet this is far too often an easy narrative bought into by white clerics in western nations who then use it as a reason to retain the status quo on LGBTQI exclusion.

Such clerics would do well to think about the legacy of colonial legislation and the continued racism that pits westerners as 'us' and Africans as 'them', a 'them' that couldn't possibly be open to the sophistication of modern western life. The reality is that the Church continues to covertly sponsor this divide, whilst enabling white hatemongers to fuel divisions within the communion and to continue to crush LGBTQI Africans. Of course, the example of LGBTQI inclusion in post-apartheid South Africa also runs a coach and horses through the lazy stereotyping of Africa as being a single culture, rather than a continent larger than the USA, China and Brazil combined. If we are to continue as an Anglican Communion, then we surely need to be honest in our discussions about where we believe Christianity ends and culture begins and have these conversations in the open with those with whom we disagree, of whatever nation, tongue or culture. Refusing to have these conversations with

---

[7] Discussion can be found in Brouwer, S., Gifford, P., Rose, S. D., *Exporting the American Gospel* (Abingdon: Taylor & Francis, 2013). It is frequently the case that right-wing or fundamentalist groups from the USA are found to be – at least in part – behind the funding and sponsoring of anti-LGBTQI legislation in the majority world.

[8] For example, Hoad, N., et al, eds., *Sex & Politics in South Africa* (Cape Town: Double Storey, 2005) and Chitando, E., and van Klinken, A., eds., *Christianity and Controversies over Homosexuality in Contemporary Africa* (Oxford: Routledge, 2016).

churches in Africa is patronising and, ultimately, racist.

It is time to stop demeaning clergy from majority world countries and to stop allowing them to be used as pawns by white fundamentalists. It is also time for us to start seriously addressing the economic damage that the Church of England has historically ravaged upon so many of what we now call 'brother and sister Anglicans' with warm hearts but empty hands. Our guilt over our colonial past must not and cannot be taken away with the blood of LGBTQI Africans. In our desperation not to impose our 'theological agenda', we would do well to treat those with whom we disagree with genuine respect and meet them on serious terms rather than imagine the position of each part of the Anglican Communion in Africa is the same. It is much easier to buy the words of the loud and powerful than it is to meet people on the ground and have honest conversations with them. We cannot allow 'the Communion', which so often means 'those Africans', to become the scapegoat for doing nothing for LGBTQI people. Yet that is precisely what the record of our church discussions suggests we continue to do.

Repression, then, can have a number of sources, yet it is clear that the culture of an organisation and often of wider society can drive individuals to either express or repress their thoughts, and indeed, as a corollary, their actions. It would be good if we could claim that the Church – as a place that is supposed to model and reward integrity, honesty and human flourishing – would be a place that avoided repression at all costs, and instead aimed to provide a healthy space where ideas may indeed be challenged and corrected, but where they are at least welcomed. Unfortunately, this has been shown time and again not to be the case. Not only are individuals encouraged into repression by church discussions that describe homosexuality as intrinsically disordered and even as a sin in and of itself – causing gay people to believe themselves to be sinful quite simply just for existing – but even in churches that are more accepting of LGBTQI people, the 'acts' are described as sinful, and therefore must be repressed at all costs.

We have seen previously how this is a false separation, yet this latter kind of description appears to be the most common in the Church of England. Even in churches that accept the existence of 'same-sex attraction', potential Christians are told that in order to belong to the club, they cannot have any kind of sexual contact – or at the least must repent of it. For those brought up in the Church, the levels of repression are likely to be even more intense and confused, as it is not when they come into contact with a church that calls homosexual activity sinful that the problem comes, but when they begin to recognise in themselves the fact that they may be LGBTQI whilst already being part of that church. This is a terrifying reality – because to act with an integrity to the self is in direct conflict with acting how the church community demands. This community might include family, friends, and indeed the whole social network, providing the only world-view that this young person might have had. In cases like this, the choice is between losing themselves or losing everything, yet churches continue to blithely say that they have no LGBTQI people in their congregations. Making this kind of statement is unacceptable – these churches have either turned away any LGBTQI potential Christians, or they have members who are so unable to express themselves that nobody knows their interior conflict. This is nothing short of church-enforced torture – a torture of externally imposed cognitive dissonance, which inevitably leads to psychological damage, and often consequences far more devastating than that.

Yet none of this is new. The Carmi report into the failure of Chichester Cathedral to respond to safeguarding concerns in 2004 stated:[9]

There is a need to address the confusion between homosexuality and child abuse that arises partly from

---

[9] https://safeguarding.chichester.anglican.org/documents/carmi-report/, p. 47.

the lack of openness about sexuality within the Church. This is part of a wider national issue that the Church has to address about sexuality.

The Gibb review into the sexual abuse committed by Bishop Peter Ball stated in 2017:[10]

The Church must promote an open and accepting culture in which everyone, regardless of their sexuality or their views about homosexuality, is clear about their responsibilities towards those who might be abused or who might want to raise concerns about abuse.

The Independent Inquiry into Child Sexual Abuse specifically referred to these reports, and stated:[11]

Bishop Martin Warner described a culture of fear amongst clergy insofar as discussions about sex were concerned...Lord Rowan Williams (the former Archbishop of Canterbury) said:
'Where sexuality is not discussed or dealt with openly and honestly, there is always a risk of displacement of emotions, denial and evasion of emotions, and thus a lack of any way of dealing effectively with troubling, transgressive feelings and sometimes a dangerous spiritualising of sexual attraction under the guise of pastoral concern, with inadequate selfunderstanding.'

We will return to the more culturally-oriented elements of the IICSA report in the next chapter, but it is intensely troubling that no serious work appears to have been done, beyond the launch of the entirely optional *Living in Love and Faith* discussions, to rectify this overarching narrative

[10] https://www.churchofengland.org/safeguarding/overview/news-and-views/independent-report-churchs-handling-peter-ball-case p. 61.
[11] https://www.iicsa.org.uk/reports-recommendations/publications/investigation/anglican-church.

of repression. It is a grave sin that it took a huge, external inquiry into the abuse of children to finally wake the Church of England up to even taking this step. The effects of an atmosphere of repression on the clergy and people of the Church of England – and not only those who are LGBTQI – is significant, and as we shall see, has led to shattering of lives and faith. Lord Williams succinctly and carefully highlights the key elements with which we have been concerned in this chapter – that where conversations about sexuality are repressed, feelings are displaced, and that this displacement has been sponsored by a 'dangerous spiritualising ... under the guise of pastoral concern', related to 'inadequate self-understanding'. The problem is that this self-understanding will always remain inadequate if the Church operates in an atmosphere of repression.

It is certainly true that many churches within the Church of England are now much more open to discussion of and with LGBTQI people, and indeed it is unfair to paint much of the Church of England as a place where sexuality and conversations about sex are entirely taboo. Yet it would also be naïve to suggest that even where those conversations are happening they are close – in terms of academic understanding of sexuality and gender, and in terms of openness to honest experience – to the standard that is reached in wider society. The Church remains a place that is squeamish about sex and that still appears to see sex as specific penetrative acts undertaken solely for procreation as opposed to a wide ranging physiological, sociological and behavioural phenomenon that displays and responds to social cues, encompasses vexed questions of power and vulnerability, carries with it a cultural narrative and is ultimately something that can be both fun and lifegiving or brutal and dehumanising.

The churches, though, that are even open to discussion are our examples of good practice! In many churches up and down the UK, discussion of sex remains entirely functional at best, and any sex outside marriage – and any sex that is not oriented towards childbearing – is seen as and described as intrinsically sinful. Those who do not fit into this simple paradigm are encouraged into a repression of the sexual urge and offered a definitive rejection of any good to be found in 'aberrant' sexual activity. In Chapters 4 and 5 we saw the inadequacy of this point of view, and in Part III we will develop thinking in this area further – for now, it is enough to recognise that this view of sex means that those who do not fit into this paradigm are expressly forbidden from any form of sexual activity. The effect on straight people who are not yet married is one thing; but the effect on those for whom sex will never be 'acceptable' is monstrous. By virtue of who they are – their intrinsic, unchangeable, core identity – they are told that sex is sin and the sexual urge must be repressed. There is no compromise.

It is perhaps worth thinking briefly about the sexual urge. It is not, of course, something solely found in human beings, and sex as part of the normal lifecycle is found throughout the great majority of animal species. The sexual urge doesn't necessarily end in sexual intercourse with another person – in some cases the urge may simply not be acted on, and in others it may lead to masturbation instead. Different churches have a variety of views on the acceptability or otherwise of masturbation, but ultimately this is about orgasm and the release of tension rather than what could properly be described as a relational sexual encounter. Yet for LGBQTI people who meet a non-affirming theology, it is the 'no' to relationship that is key. For these people, a relational sexual encounter is always out of reach – and it is frankly absurd that any such churches would permit masturbation, yet some do indeed do this (often described as 'the best of two evils').[12] Masturbation is a key example of sexual gratification without any relational aspect, and for churches to encourage this

---

[12]   An example is found in this website associated with the conservative evangelical Anglican Diocese of Sydney, Australia (https://christianity.net.au/questions/masturbation-a-sin).

instrumental view of sex yet deny the relational is simply a vision of deranged theology. It is here that the innate cruelty and yet total incoherence of the non-affirming position is most clearly displayed.

Gay, lesbian and bisexual people – in fact, all people, if we are to follow the overwhelming evidence - have a sexuality that cannot be changed by volition or force. As we have seen, the repressive position is to refuse them any coherent relational sexuality whatsoever, simply by virtue of their being non-heterosexual. It is reasonable at this point to ask the key question – why did God allow this to happen? Even if we take the most scientific understanding of evolution and consider the necessity of genetic mutation for evolution to occur, and we recognise the genetic influence – albeit as part of a multifactorial whole – on homosexuality and hence the likelihood of its development in evolutionary genetic processes as a part of sexual function, the question remains: why did God allow those who He has called by name, and who are created in His image, to be born into a world in which they can never access a relational sexuality without being condemned to hell? If God loves us individually, then surely nobody can be flotsam in the name of the greater good? Surely nobody can have been created gay even if this is necessary to create others as straight?

We have addressed the unconvincing 'regression to the Fall' theological explanation in Part I – and it is no more convincing when we try to blame the diversity of human sexuality on the Fall in this context. As we know, sexuality appears to be a spectrum and as such, it is hard to neatly delineate that which is fallen from that which is good – it is also somewhat incoherent theology, as what we would inevitably need to argue is that it is the entire sexuality of certain people that is 'fallen' (i.e. those who are attracted to those of the same sex), which raises more theological questions than it answers. This leads us back to the problem – why has God created LGBTQI people who are intrinsically unable to access relational sexuality? Are we really to believe that by virtue of this accident of genes and environment, they are all called to abstinence? The fact is that there is absolutely zero evidence that LGBTQI people as a group are somehow exempt from this need as part of their journey of human flourishing. Of course, some may be – but so are some straight people. There is a glaring dissonance here between what we know about human flourishing and this non-affirming theology.[13]

Cognitive dissonance is something that LGBTQI people, and particularly those in repressive and oppressive circumstances, are used to facing.[14] Cognitive dissonance – a felt state in which thoughts, beliefs and attitudes are inconsistent – is the inevitable outcome for LGBTQI people in non-affirming churches. This cognitive dissonance is at the heart of the damaging mental health outcomes for LGBTQI Christians and is the cause of internal repression. If this inconsistency is strong, then it needs to be dealt with. The healthy way of dealing with it is openness, discovery and expression – the unhealthy is repression, which may be successful to a varying degree and for a varying amount of time. Cognitive dissonance can ultimately be resolved by adding new beliefs, changing existing beliefs, or reducing the importance of the currently held beliefs. The problem is that any resolution that is built on sand is ultimately going to come tumbling down – either in a moment of catastrophe, or in a slow bleeding out over time that destroys not only the individual but the relationships and community that surround them. Cognitive dissonance requires serious, intentional work to resolve – the problem is that non-affirming churches spend their time trying to ensure this work is not done, all in the name of 'orthodoxy'. It is too risky to challenge, let alone change beliefs, whatever the effect on the individual – and,

---

[13] We have previously seen the theological dead-end that answers that seek to box God into this particular narrative ultimately produce, for example in the writing of Ed Shaw.

[14] Some extra reading on cognitive dissonance was recommended in Chapter 4.

far too often, those psychologically damaged and ultimately victimised individuals are then used by religious leaders to justify their particular theological position.

It is here that we turn to a somewhat uncomfortable conversation around those who, in recent years, have described themselves as 'Side B', in contrast to what they call 'Side A' LGBTQI people, who believe in full relational sexuality. Side B LGBTQI people (or, as some would prefer to self-identify, same-sex attracted people) describe themselves as holding to a 'traditional' Christian ethic, although this assertion is certainly open to challenge. Side B Christians generally fit into one of three categories – they either feel compelled to commit to single celibacy, to celibate friendships or a celibate friendship with someone else, or they enter marriages with people of the opposite sex to whom they are not sexually attracted. For those outside of church circles, this position can certainly feel quite bizarre, and it is not at all clear that marrying someone to whom one is not sexually attracted whatsoever fits even remotely within a 'traditional sexual ethic'.

Side B Christians will often lament how their position is denigrated across the Christian Church. Those who are vociferously anti-gay will often target such people, not least because some Side B Christians will describe their sexuality as 'gay' and in many ways engage in some of what is perceived as cultural aspects of being gay, albeit whilst remaining celibate. Side B Christians talk of sacrifice as a high ideal, and will often see their self-denial of sexual activity as a form of sacrifice to God – indeed, some talk of betrayal and deep hurt when churches do permit same-sex sexual activity, because they see this as a denial of their own sacrifice and struggle. There is no serious evidence-based literature on the wellbeing or flourishing of such people, and it is likely that some of the coping mechanisms are likely to be sublimation rather than pure repression. Nonetheless, whilst this may be the case, the wider evidence on human flourishing does not suggest that those denying themselves in this way will be laying the groundwork for future wellbeing.

It is not the purpose of this book to cast aspersions on or make particular judgements on those who choose to live this lifestyle. It is certainly true that some Side B Christians may simply be called to a celibate lifestyle, and some may gain a great deal from celibate friendships, as many LGBTQI and straight people do both in the Church and more widely. Whether it is ethical to enter a marriage with someone of the opposite sex to whom one feels no sexual attraction and for whom sexual intercourse is solely functional – that is, for the production of children – is questionable, and given what we have discussed about human flourishing, this would appear to be a denigration rather than a high view of sex (and a limiting of the possible flourishing of the spouse). Yet the key problem with the concept of Side B is that it denies the possibility of human flourishing including relational sexuality for any LGBTQI people, and it is not clear that repression is entirely absent from such decision-making.

Side B people are often used by theological 'conservatives' to prove their point that 'same-sex attracted' people can be happy without sex, and that such people's 'sacrifice' should not be ignored by the Church. This is fundamentally disingenuous – nobody argues that sex is essential for happiness, and similarly nobody denies that such sacrifice is painful and significant and may indeed show great faith in God. However, what must be challenged is whether such sacrifice is either warranted or ethical – and it is by no means clear that it is either of these things. Whilst some Side B Christians are very vocal about their choice, it is not obvious that the choice is always one taken freely, particularly amongst less vocal Christians who would otherwise lose their entire social network and family as we discussed earlier. Indeed, a fully worked-through Christian anthropology would cast serious doubt on the appropriateness of Side B Christians to marry solely for childbearing, and far too often it is 'same-sex attracted' men who marry straight women, with the burden placed on the women to help carry this particular 'cross'. There is no evidence that enforced celibacy is beneficial to human wellbeing, and if the theology that demands such celibacy is flimsy and later falls, the psychological damage that can be done to such people is immeasurable. The concept of Side B very much suits the 'contemporary conservative' – yet at what cost to the lives of LGBTQI people who have once again been co-opted to meet others' needs?

Of course, catastrophe can occur for such individuals when previously repressive churches 'change their mind' on this topic. Because in so many places the repression of LGBQTI sexuality has been made a marker of orthodoxy, if churches decide to change or even open up the possibility of change on this topic, the outcome can be serious psychological violence done to those who have repressed and lived with cognitive dissonance for so long, leading to a feeling of betrayal, hurt, anger and lack of identity. Yet the cause of such violence is not the change itself – it is the repression that such churches had demanded in the first place. To hear a life-encompassing organisation that has demanded you not express a key part of your identity change its mind is akin to having your life ripped apart. Yet the answer cannot be to continue that edifice of repression. A far healthier way would be to have a culture of openness in the first instance, so that if individuals do indeed come to this view of what God demands, then it is one freely chosen that can withstand the changes of any church. Far too much emphasis has been placed on the immovability of the teaching of the Church, and it is from this untruth that such situations occur. The Church has already betrayed 'Side B' Christians – particularly those who are repressing themselves because this is what the Church demands – from the start, by using their identity as a pawn in ecclesial politics. Refusing a change in doctrine on the basis of not causing harm to Side B is simply a commitment to extending the harm into the lives of future LGBTQI people. It is time the churches who decry the damage done to Side B by changing doctrine turn to look in at the damage they themselves have done.

This leads us on to considering a few possible outcomes of a repressive church. The following vignettes are based on a number of real scenarios, though are anonymised as to protect the identity of the various individuals involved:

Jack is a senior clergyman in the Church of England. He grew up when sex and sexuality was never discussed. He is gay, but never had sex until a few years ago. Since a major family tragedy, he has felt that part of his sexual life reawakened and he has decided that you only live once. The problem for Jack is that he has never really learnt what a healthy sexual life is like, and he is terrified that the 'conservative' clergy in his area will find out. So he ends up befriending and then becoming far too intimate with a young member of his congregation, because then he can keep it secret. He is accused of assault, loses his job, and is a pariah.

Tim is a sixteen-year-old bisexual teenager. He falls in love with his best friend from school and they have sex. He thinks that he can talk to his vicar, who promptly demands that he repents of his sin. Tim finds it increasingly difficult to align his experience and feelings with what the church tells him to do. He develops an eating disorder and major depression, and becomes reclusive. After a few years he enters into the seminary having never really worked through his issues and the cycle begins all over again.

Rhonda is an archdeacon who has to retire early because of pervasive guilt she has about her sexuality. She has always considered herself Side B but however much she tries, she has never been able to suppress her feelings for one of her closest friends. She and her friend kiss one night, and she feels the overwhelming urge to do it again, having finally felt something in her heart for which she has longed for many years. She feels that she cannot compromise on her faith and her ministry comes to an end.

Alex went to an evangelistic course at a church. She found the whole thing very life-affirming and realised that she wanted to become a Christian. In the final session, the vicar made a comment about homosexuality. She tried to discuss this with him, but he didn't want to engage. That was the last time Alex bothered going to a church.

Mark was in his twenties when he finally accepted that he was gay. His family were very religious, and he felt totally unable to speak to them about it. He confided in one of the people in the prayer ministry team, who told him to pray about it and remain true to God. One night, he got drunk and went out on the town, ending up sleeping with a man from whom he believed he caught HIV. He was too embarrassed to talk about it and get it treated, and a few months later the anxiety about his possible HIV status and his constant feelings of guilt at church led him to put a rope around his neck and hang himself. Mark's family found out about what happened from a note he left and were so disgusted they didn't attend his funeral at the crematorium.

These are just snapshots into what repression can do to individuals within and without the leadership of the Church. LGBTQI people are particularly vulnerable at the time when they discover their own sexuality. Many impose internal repression on themselves, for fear of talking to others and facing accusations and further guilt. Others broach these conversations, and end up facing external repression. Whatever the source, the repression pushes their sexual feelings down, but not away – and it is inevitable that at some stage these will resurface. In some cases, this might only be to have a one-night stand with someone of the same sex whilst they are married to someone of the opposite sex. For others, this failure of repressive mechanisms will end up in their deaths. LGBTQI young people continue to die by suicide at an alarming rate, and in far too many cases this is related to religion.[15]

Others will end up with such immature emotional and relational lives that they become a danger to others – not because they are LGBTQI, but because they have been told that their very nature is disordered and end up deeply damaging themselves. Some will abuse others, and some will have confused sexual boundaries with and from others. Many will end up with mental health problems and destroyed relationships. Many will walk away from faith altogether. It doesn't have to be this way.

It is abundantly clear that repression is not a healthy form of living, in church or otherwise. Our churches should be places where the Holy Spirit breathes on us and gives us life – places where we find courage, love, joy, and hope in the life, death and resurrection of Jesus Christ. It is for this reason that we must move beyond the evil of repression. At the very least, we must become places of hospitality in which openness about human flourishing and relational living becomes the norm. We must become places where we openly talk about, rather than hide, our difficulties and challenges. To be such a place is to value listening and discerning above lecturing and determining.

The argument of this book is that this is only the tip of the iceberg. Not only do we need to let in the fresh air of truth and love into the atmosphere of our churches, but we need to seriously consider the damage we are doing by repressing the bodies and souls of LGBTQI people too. LGBTQI people are people of relationship as much as straight people are, and denial of this can only lead to loss. The repression of this part of the self seems entirely counter to a life lived in God, and the overwhelming evidence suggests only negative

---

[15] For example, Lytle M. C., et al, 'Association of Religiosity with Sexual Minority Suicide Ideation and Attempt', *American Journal of Preventative Medicine* (2018) 54 (5) pp. 644-651, with a good summary available at The Trevor Project (https://www.thetrevorproject.org/research-briefs/religiosity-and-suicidality-among-lgbtq-youth/).

consequences, from cognitive dissonance to mental and physical break-down, all in the name of the God of love. It is hard to believe this is what God wants for His people, and it is hard to see this reflected in His divine nature. We shall think more about relational sexual expression in Section 3, but for now we turn to what a turn towards a culture of openness might do for our churches.

7

OPENNESS OR
ERASURE

The culture of any organisation is key to its success, however that success might be measured. Whilst far too much discourse in recent years has uncritically adopted the language and aims of secular organisations and applied them to the Church of England, nonetheless it is essential that we do have some understanding of what successful might look like in this context. Churches are ultimately most successful when they most closely resemble in their outward expression that which is at their core – indeed, where the cognitive dissonance we have discussed is at a minimum in the life and witness of the Church. Of course, as in any organisation inhabited and managed by human beings, there will always be internal contradiction, hypocrisy and double standards – this is inevitable, and any claim of perfection in this regard is blasphemous. Nonetheless, churches have a responsibility and a vocation to strive for truth and integrity, and to be places of tangible encounter with the beauty of the Gospel of Christ and the Kingdom of God that they are called to embody.

The culture of a church, therefore, whether the Church corporate or in its local manifestation, matters, because it is the culture which – in a dance of reciprocation – both sets and exemplifies the rules of engagement. The biblical witness is plentiful in highlighting those things that are of the Spirit and thus central to the calling of the Church, and likewise those attitudes which ultimately lead to malaise and decay. It should not be a huge surprise that the biblical witness and human knowledge in this area point in the same direction – indeed, it only becomes a problem when the determination to employ the God-world dichotomy outweighs our willingness to see the human sciences as a gift from God. At the heart of any church that is seeking after truth – in 'love, joy, peace, patience, kindness, generosity, faithfulness, gentleness, and self-control' (Galatians 5:22-23) – is integrity, honesty, openness and a listening ear. It is then that Christians do 'not become conceited, competing against one another, envying one another' (Galatians 5:26), and instead the Church becomes the kind of place that is not only infused with the Holy Spirit but also shines outwards as a place where God has made his dwelling place.

This is the difficulty with loving our neighbour as ourself in the context of loving one another as Christ loved us – it requires a fundamental and radical honesty, not only with our neighbour but with ourselves as well. This is seriously hard work, because it starts with introspection and asks us to ask very challenging questions of our own motivations and desires. Sometimes those very things are beyond our grasp if we do not seek help from others – and these others should most certainly include those in the Church, and not least in the confessional. Yet if that church is a place where honesty is a dirty word (or, perhaps worse, where honesty is consistently compromised by wink-wink, nudge-nudge), the risk becomes that the more we feel we are being introspective, the more we are gaslit and manipulated into a situation where we question that which is real. A church in which openness about LGBTQI matters is not only frowned upon but actively shunned, however unconsciously, is a church that is failing to 'equip the saints for the work of ministry, for building up the body of Christ' (Ephesians 4:12) and a church which is bound to fail. It is also a church that is bound to do damage to the flock and, as we shall see, become a place of moribund mission and ministry.

For LGBTQI people, the reality is that the Church is often the last place to go for open conversations or guidance on sexuality; indeed, LGBTQI people are infrequently seen as the saints that need building up and equipping. Historically, the Church has been a place that is so ignorant of the topic that it has had nothing but condemnation to offer; in recent years, a culture of fear has complemented this, making the Church inhospitable and a place of erasure. Of course, pockets of good practice and healthy culture exist in some parishes, yet at an institutional level the Church of England cannot claim to be anything other than institutionally homophobic, mired as it is in a refusal to speak honestly on this issue. It is a far too common occurrence that bishops and others say in private what they dare not say in public, justified with a broad appeal to unity and to the need for appeasement for those of different theological opinions. The LGBTQI 'issue' is too hot to handle, and so a blancmange of mealymouthed warm words and lukewarm half-smiles is offered instead of anything remotely resembling theological integrity. LGBTQI people, meanwhile, are acceptable collateral.

This is a fundamentally dishonest position, for several reasons. In the first instance, it is an open secret that there is a financial incentive to saying nothing of substance. In the Church of England, there is an unspoken belief – which is to some extent justified – that were these conversations and affirming bishops' genuine opinions to come out into the open, then the money would dry up, coming as it often does from churches who appear to have staked their entire Christian vision on vehement opposition to LGBTQI sexual expression. For an institution that is supposed to be built on truth and not mammon, this is an extraordinary position to take, yet it is demonstrably the one taken. Of course, it would be foolish to imagine that the Church of England would not suffer if this money dried up, but nonetheless the current position is akin to unspoken blackmail. It is unfathomable that bishops – those chosen to provide oversight and moral leadership – are so unable to face this issue head on in a remotely public fashion, whilst many are willing to lament it behind closed doors. Not naming this is a shameful act and a refusal to do so simply empowers those who seek to use finances as a way to entomb the Church in their particular interpretation of scripture.

Another argument, again somewhat spurious, is that the only growing churches are those that exhibit theologies that demand LGBTQI repression. Not only is this not borne out by the facts,[1] but it is a significant step to move from correlation to causation – something senior church leaders would understand more if their grasp of the scientific method were more sound. The Bishop of St Asaph, in an astoundingly moving speech to the Governing Body of the Church in Wales during their recent consideration of same-sex blessings, got to the heart of this when he spoke of the 'depth of your watering holes' rather than 'your boundaries' when addressing the numerical growth of 'conservative' churches in his diocese and province.[2] There is doubtless church growth occurring in conservative circles and it is wrong to discount all of this because of their position on LGBTQI inclusion, but it is essential that some level of critical analysis is applied to it, rather than the assertions of such congregations that young people and other new Christians support their anti-LGBTQI stance being blithely accepted as Gospel. No serious sociological study backs up these assertions, and yet they keep being made and seemingly imbibed by those in positions of power.

Later chapters will comment further on whether 'bums on pews' is really the right – or at least sole – metric for the building

[1] Limited reputable studies are available, but the argument is commonly made that, anecdotally, more 'conservative' churches are growing. That this is related to their views on sexuality is questionable; similarly, it is by no means clear that numerical growth in attendance is the same as growth in the faith, and the longevity of membership in such churches (as opposed to fast turnaround of new believers) is infrequently reported. An interesting discussion, written by Darren Slade of the Global Centre for Religious Research, is found here: https://www.gcrr.org/post/correlation-is-not-causation-why-theology-is-not-what-makes-churches-grow.

[2] A summary and recording of the Synod is found here: https://www.churchinwales.org.uk/en/about-us/governing-body/highlights-september-2021/.

up of the body of Christ. At this stage, however, it is important to ask why senior clergy continue to avoid being open about their own views. It is an unfair joke, frequently made, that at episcopal ordination one of the key elements is the removal of the spine, but there are very serious questions that need to be asked when bishops who have previously been vocally pro-LGBTQI feel unable or are unwilling to continue to speak in this way once they have been elevated to the episcopate. Ultimately, that this is the case casts a very significant shadow on the culture of the Church. For the most senior clergy in the Church to feel unable to speak suggests a rot at the centre of the organisation – a rot that inevitably trickles down to those in positions of authority and right down to the worshipper in the pews. When the culture at the top is toxic, then the culture throughout the organisation is bound to be affected. The sad reality is that this is openly discussed amongst senior clergy – and yet such discussion is never aired in public, or in a way that could actually lead to change. Yet change it must, if the Church is to survive, let alone thrive, in the contemporary world where transparency and honesty are more valued than ever before.

It should be stated clearly at this point that highlighting this failure in the machinery of the current episcopate is not to cast aspersions on individuals or to suggest that there is necessarily a simple solution. Many bishops appear personally affronted when presented with evidence of systemic malfunction, and a war of words is unhelpful in getting to grips with the underlying problem. The willingness of some bishops to speak out on LGBTQI issues, yet only once they have left office, nevertheless points to a structural problem in how episcopacy is currently practiced in the Church.[3] Discomfort discussing matters sexual is hardly new,

---

[3] An example is here: https://retiredbishopsletter.wordpress.com/letter/. That being said, some of the signatories, including Bishop Peter Selby, did speak out during their ecclesial career. Of particular interest is Peter Selby's book – *Belonging: Challenge to a Tribal Church* (London: SPCK, 1991) – which is prophetic and remains entirely relevant to the current position of the Church of England.

in the Church or outside of it, although it is disappointing that the Church – which should be able to discuss and seek to understand anything in the entire creation of God if it is truly to be the Church – is lagging so far behind many other institutions that have had to lose their squeamishness for the sake of effective functioning. It is doubtless extremely challenging to be a bishop, or any senior clergy, in the modern world, given the huge calls on time and the need to constantly update oneself across the whole gamut of church life, and it is also the case that the reasons for the current malaise are multiple and complex.

Yet it is also unacceptable to turn a blind eye to this failure; it is demonstrably the case that the bishops of the Church of England have lost the ability to speak about sexuality in a way that models integrity and honesty for the rest of the Church. This is a serious problem not only because it suggests the episcopate is somewhat compromised, but because it speaks to a broken culture of the Church that puts bishops in this position. It is clearly not the case that upon becoming a bishop one's entire position on these matters changes; rather, it is generally felt that to be open is to run too great a risk to the unity of the Church. This gives a very damaging picture of the wider church culture that both leads to and cultivates this inability to speak and overgrowth of fear. As clergy and laity, we cannot lay the blame solely at the door of bishops – we must have some introspection as to how things have gotten to this stage.

That there is silence over LGBTQI issues is demonstrable, yet it is surely not the only element of church life in which bishops' ability to speak out honestly is compromised – these things rarely occur in a vacuum. It is, then, the entire church culture that needs airing out, although in a way that tackles the root causes of these problems rather than simply places a sticking plaster. Much has been made of tackling 'clericalism' in church circles, and it is often the most ardent opponents of LGBTQI sexual expression that speak most about making the church 'more relevant' by throwing out clerical garments and introducing more relaxed forms of worship. It is interesting, of course, that such churches see LGBTQI inclusion as 'of the culture' and highlight their opposition as a counter-cultural witness, whilst apparently not recognising that worship in the form of an informal pop concert is about as 'of the culture' as can be! Yet the serious point is that despite this apparent deliberate attempt to reduce clericalism, it appears that it is the peripheral and the superficial that has been targeted, rather than the underlying attitudes that lead to the rotten culture. In far too many churches, the view of the leadership is not only unchallenged but unchallengeable, meaning that the real, lived experience of the people in the pews is always subordinate to the abstractions of the man (and it is usually a man) in the pulpit. Churches continue to talk about 'sound biblical preaching' in which the congregation are viewed as receiver and the preacher as giver, reinforcing the culture of erasure and leading to a homogenous view of Christianity that fails to take into account the reality and variation of human lives.

It is not at all clear, then, that many local church communities are much healthier than the sickness found in the centre, and the way that sex and sexuality is discussed and embraced (or otherwise) is frequently a totem that signals such putrefaction. It is doubtless the case that what can be said here about bishops might particularly apply to the self-appointed leaders of those church groups that vociferously opposed LGBTQI inclusion. As we shall discuss, a large growing church does not necessarily indicate a healthy church, and whilst certain leadership methodologies and behaviours may lead to one of these options, they will often directly rebuff the other. A serious level of introspection is required here, but the risk of this introspection is that the certainties that previously held might be washed away, revealing the sand rather than the rock. Nonetheless, a culture whose core is rotten needs a new core in order to survive, let alone thrive. Perhaps that is what is needed in parts of today's church.

Discussions about LGBTQI people are, indeed, often a proxy for conversations about sex and sexuality more generally. It is outside the scope of this book to delve into the complicated arguments around male headship and other sex-determined Christian anthropologies, but it is certainly true that the body – and most particularly the non-straight male body – has proven a nexus for control throughout history and across different cultures, and thus sex itself is often a proxy for a much wider conversation about power and vulnerability. That Christianity has not managed to throw off the very human lust for power is disappointing but not entirely unpredictable, and we will interrogate what this means for the Church more in the following chapter. However, the key point for our discussion here is that any sickness in this area is indicative of a wider cultural malaise, and it is essential to try to determine how we have gotten here and how we might get away from it if we are to help develop a church culture that is ultimately life-giving for all of God's children, LGBTQI or otherwise.

We discussed above some of the reasons posited for a silence of the bishops of this issue, both of which relate to a realpolitik ultimately driven by fear. There are frequently calls for bishops to show more courage in this area, and it is reasonable to press this point. It is certainly the case that huge numbers of LGBTQI people will not go near the Church because of its hostility, or silence in the face of hostility, towards them, and it is somewhat shameful that LGBTQI people continue to appear to be seen as an acceptable sacrifice in the name of unity. Gregory Cameron, the Bishop of St Asaph referred to earlier in this chapter, spoke to this point when he summed up his speech in favour of LGBTQI inclusion, saying:

Dear friends who are committed to a particular understanding of the Bible, you will always be welcome in the Church in Wales and we will learn so much from you. But not I'm afraid at the price of betraying my gay and lesbian brothers and sisters. If they want to seek God's blessing, I will not forbid them.[4]

Unfortunately, to date, there have been very few Church of England bishops (with the exception of the Bishop of Liverpool, Paul Bayes, and the Bishop of Buckingham, Alan Wilson) who have been willing to be so publicly explicit or, indeed, welcoming. It is extremely worrying that a culture of fear can exert this level of control over the very people called to shepherd God's people. In Section 1, the calls for softly-softly, yet ultimately ineffective, approaches were considered, as was the ease of making such pronouncements if one has a spouse with whom to return home, with the approval and warmth of friends, family and church. It is doubtless the case that for some bishops, and indeed others in the Church, the urgency and human cost of saying nothing is still not recognised, with the inclusion of LGBTQI people seen as a lower priority than many other pressing issues.

Yet there is one group of clergy, and bishops, for whom this issue is both a priority, and yet also an issue which instils absolute terror – LGBTQI clergy. We shall see in the next chapter what the current Church of England position is and what this means about our church, but for now it is enough to know that for some clergy in some dioceses, the simple fact of being LGBTQI is enough to end a ministry. Clergy infrequently talk about their ministry as a career, but it is nonetheless important to enunciate that promotion is a very real opportunity for some clergy, and is not intrinsically at odds with vocation – in fact, it may well act in conjunction with it. Yet for LGBTQI clergy, to 'get on' in the Church often means hiding one's entire sense of self, and indeed often either repressing one's wish for

[4]   See Footnote 2 above.

a relationship or, just as harmfully, hiding the very person who you love. Even if LGBTQI clergy are open about who they love – and we have seen the appalling treatment of those who are honest, like Jeffrey John – then they are expected to live a half-in and half-out life, having to hide part of who they are around judgemental colleagues and congregations, and constantly measuring how 'open' to be against a host of prejudices launched in their direction.

Worst still is the situation around sex. At present, the Church of England's position is that sex is for marriage only, and because it is not possible for clergy or ordinands of the Church of England to enter into same-sex marriages, they are by virtue of this ruling not allowed to have sex with their partners. Given all we have said previously about repression and the damage that this can do to individuals, this is an extremely destructive place to put such clergy in. However, that is to say nothing of the individuals with whom they have chosen to live their lives, who in the great majority of cases do not feel a call to celibacy but are being indirectly commanded by the Church to decide whether to fulfil their own relational needs or to enable the obedience of their clergy partner to these pernicious rules. It is abundantly clear that this current position is neither sustainable nor just, and yet the Church continues to enforce a document written in 1991, *Issues in Human Sexuality*, that is both inconsistent and incoherent, and is an insult to the intelligence of clergy and laity alike. This document does not warrant any serious investigation at this stage, except to state that its application by the current Church of England is to prevent gay (or to use its bizarre language, 'homophile') sexual relationships amongst the clergy. That human knowledge in this area has progressed since 1991 is something of an understatement, and *Issues* cannot be described as cutting edge even according to the standards of 1991. To continue to apply this as the gold standard of Christian teaching is to provide a pointer as to the critical nature of the Church's illness.[5]

Given all that we know about human relationships and the place of sexual behaviour within them, to allow clergy relationships that would normally embody relational sexuality, yet explicitly forbidding that very sexuality, is both cruel and highly inconsistent, once again highlighting the problem that occurs when the sexual 'act' is considered as though it is separable from its relational association. The reality, once again a reality that is not spoken about because of the culture of fear, is that many clergy are simply flouting the rules and engaging in sexual relationships. This is an entirely understandable and reasonable response to a rule that is fundamentally dishonest, obedience being promised to the bishop in things 'lawful and honest'.[6] Yet the fact that LGBTQI clergy are having sexual relationships, yet are forced into dishonesty by this culture of secrecy, shows how corrupt and how ultimately corrupting it can be.

In the first instance, clergy who cannot have sex and who would lose their license for doing so (or rather, for being honest about it) within the context of a loving, monogamous relationship cannot speak openly and truthfully about the life-giving effects of relational sexuality. Whilst it is certainly true that the voice of the laity is better heard in the contemporary church, nonetheless this means that an entire group of clergy's voices are not heard in conversations amongst the

[5] That *Issues* remains the gold standard for clergy discipline and behaviour in the Church of England is a sign of the paralysis that lies within the system, the lack of leadership, and willingness to ignore the protestations of LBGTQI people. There are numerous examples of the poor thinking involved in this document. The section on bisexuality (Section 5:8) appears to misunderstand bisexuality and suggest that bisexual people will be having multiple sexual relationships concurrently with people of different sexes; meanwhile, the Section 4 – The Phenomenon of Homosexual Love – is not only hopelessly out of date, but even asks whether, were a gay gene discovered, it would be ethical to 'eliminate' it. Not only does this kind of thinking lead us down a rabbit hole (one might think of the 'natural law' arguments and ask what precisely we mean by naturally occurring) but it is also gratuitously offensive and dangerous. That *Issues* remains in place is a scandal.

[6] As required in the Oath of Canonical Obedience for clergy.

clergy, for fear of losing a license – and with it, for stipendiary clergy, a house, salary and pension. Whilst the financial risk for non-stipendiary is less, nonetheless the more senior an appointment in the Church, the more likely it is to be full time, meaning that those who can most afford to be more honest are least likely to be near the centre of power. All this added together means that the conversation is naturally skewed away from honesty and lived experience towards repression and silence. This is the very definition of erasure.

A further, and more worrying, trend is towards a culture of 'anything goes' sexuality, amongst LGBTQI clergy but more widely as well. At present, the Church's position is that sex between a monogamous same-sex couple is totally unacceptable and is an aberration that goes against God's law. For LGBTQI clergy and laity who hear (and believe) this kind of language, the benefits and importance of lifelong monogamy are totally abrogated – the relationship is not valued whatsoever if sex is involved, because that sex is fundamentally wrong. It is not a huge leap from this kind of position to one in which sex is seen entirely as a bodily act in and of itself, as a letting off of steam or a fulfilling of an urge, and as something about which to always feel guilty and of which to always repent.

Sex, thus, becomes entirely functional rather than relational, and begins to take on that very definition of 'genital activity' that is so roundly condemned. Sex and relationship are ripped apart, and because of this, all sex, either within a relationship or otherwise, becomes loaded with the same moral worth as sex within a loving, committed relationship. It is, simply, 'gay sex', and it is all unacceptable. Because it is all unacceptable, then it all becomes equally acceptable, and it is from here that we enter a very grey area indeed. At the very least, sexual partners are treated as 'it' and nothing more, and yet over time the self is also degraded through the loss of relationality. Relationships are easily broken when sex is forbidden with the beloved and the sexual urge is 'discharged' elsewhere. Yet still darker avenues exist in a world in which all gay sex is wrong, because it becomes easier to excuse dreadful actions when they are all part of a great ocean of 'wrong-ness'.

This is a dangerous place to end up, and it is important to state that there is nothing inevitable on the individual level about ending up in this place. The great majority of LGBTQI clergy do not commit abuse, and there is no link whatsoever between homosexuality and abuse. Nor is this an attempt to explain away or excuse the appalling behaviour of abusers. Nobody is forced into committing abuse, and it is collusion with – or co-option of – such a culture that leads to these appalling cases of sexual violence. It is worth seriously considering whether an organisation that had a healthier approach to sex would offer such safe harbour to abusers, and it is for this reason – amongst a multitude of others – that the question of repressive sexuality cannot continue to be kicked down the road.

It is the Church's culture, then, with which we are particularly concerned, and it is demonstrably the case that a culture of secrecy, half-truths, wink-wink, nudge-nudge, inevitably leads to a culture of unhealthy sexuality, and with it and in some cases, not only actions of great depravity, but a veneer of acceptability that would be blown away in the light of day. It is not homosexuality that leads to this place, but the forcing of sexuality into a repressive shadowland and the development of a culture that not only enables, but actively encourages, duplicity. It is a direct outcome of the sickness at the heart of the Church – and the argument that suggests that if people simply abided by the Church's forbidding of sexual relationships for LGBTQI people then this wouldn't happen is an argument that completely misses the point. It is in the context of terrible rules that this situation has developed, and it is unacceptable to continue to point the finger of blame at those who are already victimised by systematic persecution by the Church. It is the result of ignorance and prejudice that leads to these kinds of terrible outcome and that is the very ignorance and prejudice that lead to the imposition of such unjust rules in the first place.

Yet, once again – just like in the previous chapter – this is not a new insight. Returning to the IICSA report:[7]

> It is no surprise that a culture of secrecy and denial was present amongst clergy who were LGBTQIA. Bishop Warner told us that the late 19th century saw the development of an AngloCatholic subculture, which offered a safe space for homosexual clergy and laity alike. Mr Colin Perkins helpfully set out the hypothetical example of a gay priest, keen to follow his calling but reluctant to endure a life of celibacy. In the cultural context of AngloCatholicism, this resulted in what Mr Perkins described as an *'overt conservatism and a covert liberalism, which will generate a lot of secrecy'.*

The report is clear in that this is not solely an Anglo-Catholic problem, not least because the culture the repression engenders in the wider church can lead to very bad outcomes. Indeed, whilst different parts of the Church managed the repressive position differently, in more recent years it has been in conservative evangelical churches that homosexuality has been most aggressively repressed, whilst many of a 'conservative' Anglo-Catholic bent continue to sponsor an environment in which code-words like 'lodger' are used in order to assert that everything is 'above board'. Both of these subcultures, and mixtures of the two – neither of which are safe or healthy – contribute to a wider whole in which prejudice and repression form a heady brew that ultimately contribute to a deeply unhealthy church culture.

> Reverend Hunt asserted that *'the need to be discreet about one's sexuality has enabled those who wish to abuse to do so with some impunity'.*

---

[7] The following quotations are from https://www.iicsa.org.uk/reports-recommendations/publications/investigation/anglican-church.

In addition, we hear of a witness to the report who had 'an internal conflict [about homosexuality] which he had no desire to confront', and he therefore 'reacted to the tension by refusing to acknowledge that homosexual activity existed. He avoided the issue altogether by erecting a mental barrier or, to use the common phrase, by turning a blind eye.'

> The Carmi review summarised this process as *selective blindness towards behaviour caused by intolerance of homosexuality, but awareness that this was not acceptable and a consequent suspension of judgement to the behaviour of those perceived to be homosexuals'.*
>
> Lord Williams summarised this as *'a rather paradoxical consequence of the traditional view of homosexuality within the Church; you want to overcompensate a bit for it'.*

That there was rot in the heart of the culture of the Church of England is clearly attested to, not only in these brief selected phrases from the report but running as a thread throughout it. A culture in which homosexuality is neither understood nor spoken about openly is a culture that is ultimately unsafe not only for LGBTQI people trying to live healthy and happy lives – who come under unwarranted suspicion – but also those who are vulnerable to sexual abuse through a blind eye being turned. The blind eye being turned is directly related to this lack of comprehension and lack of openness – one evil leading to another. Yet it is worrying that those interviewed for the report seem to believe the culture of the Church has undergone a 'striking change ... over the last two decades':

> For instance, Lord Williams noted that *'an environment in which, perhaps, thirty or forty years ago, clergy would have been afraid to talk openly about their sexuality if it was minority sexuality ... that's largely disappeared'.* The topic of clergy sexuality has been openly debated in Synod. It is also the subject of a proposed teaching document on sexuality and learning resources about human identity

and sexuality. However, as Lord Williams commented, the Church's growing discomfort with traditional closeted attitudes may have contributed to the reluctance of some individuals to deal appropriately with abuse.

This, frankly, appears to be grossly over-stating the reality. Whilst there may indeed be more conversations about sexuality at synodical level, on the ground absolutely nothing has changed in terms of the rules that set the scene. Clergy continue to be forced into dishonesty or repression, and healthy sexuality is discussed, at most, at the abstract level. The 'cultural hiding place' identified in IICSA remains, and the behaviour of repressed and repressive clergy and laity – like those we met in the last chapter – continue to blight the ministry and mission of the Church.

Once again, this is emphatically not an argument against solidarity amongst LGBTQI clergy (and indeed laity), and gay subcultures are not necessarily bad in and of themselves. Yet any subculture that is forcibly hidden away, and thus is not permitted or encouraged to dialogue with the mainstream of thought, opinion and practice, always runs the risk of becoming something genuinely aberrant and unhealthy. It may seem mildly embarrassing that some clergy continue to refer to their sexual partners as their 'lodger' or 'special friend', but over time the damage this kind of obfuscation and half-truth can contribute to – to the individual, to their partner, to their relationship, to their ministry, to their integrity and to the culture of the local and wider church – must not be underestimated. To be blunt, this kind of behaviour would be condemned in straight clergy – yet we appear to give it the Church's blessing for those who are LGBQTI, and when such a culture is found to contribute to a wider unhealthy sexual ethic, we blame those LGBTQI clergy once again. It is certainly time for LGBTQI clergy to stop colluding with this kind of culture, but straight Christians need to do the bulk of the work in making this a safe choice.

Earlier in this chapter, we were critical of the current episcopate and their seeming inability or unwillingness to call out and reshape the unhealthy culture of the contemporary church. However, there is one group of bishops who are between a rock and a hard place – those who are LGBQTI. There are barely any openly LGBTQI bishops in the Church of England, with the Bishop of Grantham, Nicholas Chamberlain, having been forcibly outed as being in a Civil Partnership in 2016, and 'conservatives' continue to argue against the appointment of celibate gay bishops for reasons which are neither coherent nor obvious, given the official line of 'celibacy good, sex bad'. Yet it is common knowledge that there are a number of LGBTQI bishops currently serving: some of them are openly so to those who they trust and for some it is something of an open secret. Yet it is striking that despite the Bishop of Grantham's outing, not a single other gay bishop came out publicly to show solidarity or support him. This is testament to the crippling levels of fear that exist amongst the episcopate – it is unimaginable that for any other major facet of someone's identity this level of secrecy would remain. Of course, it would be a prophetic move were some LGBTQI bishops to take a stand and be willing to take the risk of being open.

As a church, this is what we are doing to our bishops, our clergy, and our people. No amount of 'wellbeing charter' is going to resolve that. At present we have a culture that is designed to erase the voices and lives of LGBTQI people, keeps them in constant fear and leads to an ever-spiralling cycle of inhumanity. It is not only LGBTQI people who are hurt either, for such an attitude blights any conversation on sex, sexuality, relationships, and love, as we shall see when we consider the current debates around marriage. We are all combatants in a fight between the opposing forces of integrity and dishonesty within church discourse and structures, and we see the contemporary outcome of a church that has far too much of the latter and far too little of the former. The culture of our church matters because it informs and colours everything we do and are. Having explored the effect on individuals and on culture, we now move to consider the effect on the wider ministry and mission of the Church.

8

VULNERABILITY OR POWER

So far, our discussions have primarily focused on the damage done to the Church by the current position on LGBTQI issues by being intentionally introspective. We have seen what happens to individuals who are trapped in a cycle of repression and what that can do to the wider culture of the Church. The more open LGBTQI people are, the more precarious their place in the Church, and the more the forces of repression shout them down. Yet the other side of the coin leads to the shadowlands of denial, which fosters an unhealthy spirituality for individual and institution alike. In this chapter, we will take more of a bird's-eye view and ask what the out-workings of the current Church of England picture looks like in practice. The arguments on LGBTQI people are frequently made in the abstract, and it is because of this that church leaders can continue to call for more time to 'debate' the 'issue'. The reality on the ground can be devastating.

In this chapter, we will see how frequently this is a debate which ultimately boils down to power. The Bible has much to say about power and vulnerability, and the track record of the Church in its handling of LGBTQI issues (and engaging with LGBTQI people) does not reflect well on its relationship with power. As with so much we have considered, it is infrequently the case – with some exceptions – that there is a deliberate attempt to abuse power relationships. One of the great tragedies of the Church's reprehensible behaviour in matters of sexuality is that there are many people within the Church who genuinely believe what they are doing is right, not only for the health of the Church but also to save the souls of LGBTQI people who they believe are bound for Hell if they are sexually active. This may not be the language of the Church of England but scratching beneath the surface readily exposes such attitudes. Yet for many of these people, the missing ingredient in their spiritual lives appears to be introspection. A failure to pay serious attention to power dynamics is often at the heart of this – a failure to challenge one's own assumptions and to be closed to challenge, and, often, to refuse to countenance the possibility of being wrong. This is often seen in the language used about 'biblical truth', with the almost comical line 'the Bible is very clear' being a key symptom of this problem.

Arguing that the Bible is very clear is often a proxy for one of several underlying beliefs. The simplest of these is a belief that we really do know the mind of God. Putting a charitable bent on this, people may argue that they have read extensively or have prayed carefully over the texts and cannot in good conscience come to any other decision on the topic. This is not a line that is reserved solely to matters of sexuality – it is astounding how 'clear' the Bible is on a number of different topics, and often in rather contradictory ways! We saw the risk of using the Bible in this way in Chapters 2 and 3 – at the very least, this kind of statement needs to be qualified with a level of contingency, although the common argument against that is the spectre of relativism. If nothing is clear, it goes, then we have simply bought into postmodern relativistic theology, in which there is no truth but my truth. This is a facile argument – the entire history of Christian thought has been an attempt to know God more closely and carefully, from a whole host of different angles and with built in contingencies along the way. Even Aquinas recognised this, when in later life – after writing one of the most breath-taking works of theology that continues to inform and influence today – he said, 'All that I have written seems to me so much straw after the things that have been revealed to me.' Having some humility is not an open door to relativism.

That is not the same, of course, as suggesting that there are no things on which the Bible appears to speak with more clarity than others – and as we saw earlier, it is primarily through taking the Bible on its own terms and understanding it as a dialogical and narrative record of revelation that these things become clear. Yet there remains a great risk to using the Bible as a weapon. It is entirely legitimate for those in academic study of the Bible to make strong claims about their biblical interpretations, in whichever field of study, but the Church is not the academy and academic understandings need to be tested in the fire of the life of the Church. We may hypothetically prove beyond reasonable doubt that particular Greek words used in the epistles really do refer to consensual sexual acts between two men (although such a claim is highly dubious), yet this does not immediately mean that the Christian church must oppose homosexuality in all its forms. It is absolutely essential that we continue to strive for the most viable meaning of different parts of scripture, but this does not provide a *eureka* moment – instead, this academic study enriches the life of the Church through dialogue. Academics who are also clergy need to be much more mindful of this – it is easy to preach one's own academic work rather than the saving Gospel of Jesus Christ. Of course, the two may not be worlds apart, but it is a slippery slope to ruin when we start preaching our interpretation as the immovable and unchallengeable Gospel of Christ.

Yet we must also be careful of always giving too charitable an interpretation to the pronouncements of those who claim to know the mind of God. In the Church, like elsewhere, there remain people whose lack of introspection and whose privilege leads them to quite genuinely believe that they know better and know more than others, and that it is their right and even calling to ensure that their interpretation is not only heard but enforced. It does not come as a huge surprise that such people often share similar characteristics, being white, male, heterosexual, cis-gendered and well off. Such characteristics do not inevitably lead to this kind of behaviour, but in the world of today, they help – particularly when coupled with a lack of introspection. This is an outright abuse of power and authority, and one that the Church should stamp on before it damages more souls. Yet such people are often lauded because of their preaching or leadership – both of which often rely on charisma and natural authority so easily embodied by such people (although, of course, this says nothing of the quality of either). It is usually the case that the Bible is clear – in their minds – on the things that do not define them, thus they can opine on the role of women, LGBTQI people, racial equality, all without any risk to themselves. Often this is not much more than baptised prejudice, patriarchy and heterosexualism. As we shall see below, this thread of thinking has a strong foothold in the Church – an institution in which it should be much more uncomfortable, and much more challenged, than it presently is.

A final category of those for whom the Bible is very clear is those who have been told it is so. For these Christians, the clarity of the Bible in opposition to LGBTQI people is often intrinsically linked with their Christian faith and may have been made one of the foundational beliefs to sign up to when 'becoming a Christian'. This carries with it quite some risk, not least in a missional sense, as any change in thinking on this topic is likely to shake these foundations. Once again, those to blame for this kind of situation are those who – in most cases quite wittingly – choose to define the faith of their converts in this way, or who propagate the idea that loyalty to the institution of the Church should trump one's own integrity. We have seen possible disastrous outcomes where loyalty is placed above honesty already in this part of the book – yet this is a common refrain when people (often unaffected themselves directly) speak about being unable to go against the 'settled view' of the Church on matters of sexuality. As we described in the first few chapters, any church that refuses challenge, and holds onto particular traditions for their own sake is not a church filled with the lifeblood of the Gospel. A serious and honest church must see challenge as part and parcel of its own search for God. That something has always been the case and accepted is not a valid argument in and of itself in the face of demonstrable, clear, evidenced opposition (thinking again of our example of evolution). To refuse to grapple – or to fall back on 'but the Church says' – is to refuse the risk of grace.

A closed attitude may work to ensure a club mentality and hence a more cohesive early few years in the Christian fold, but this is ultimately disastrous when cognitive dissonance rears its head. This cognitive dissonance is not just for the LGBTQI people for whom such an initiation into Christianity is little short of violence – it will also be felt by those whose friends, family, or even colleagues, are LGBTQI, and who are pushed to the place where something must give, either their relationship with these people or their faith. It does not need to be this way, and it is extraordinary that the Church would be an organisation that drives people to choose to break relationships that are in all other ways life-giving. It seems extremely unlikely that God would ask this of us.

This highlights the importance of the stewardship of power in the Church. Talk of immortal souls, God's judgement and opining on morality mixed with an institutional structure, a club mentality and somewhat unaccountable leadership is a heady mix that can easily lead to emotional abuse. Too little discussion still takes place about this kind of danger, and we are all too easily lulled into a position where 'diversity of church tradition' is presented as a barrier to tackling what would, in any other institution, be seen as serious breaches of professional and ethical obligations. It should be clearly and unambiguously stated that this kind of emotional manipulation is unacceptable within an organisation that is supposed to be about openness and freely chosen faith. One of the most worrying elements is that this kind of manipulation often occurs when young people are at their most vulnerable, finding their feet at school or university, in the middle of a period of their life in which hormones are raging and psychological development is at its most malleable – and potentially open to damage. The following example is an anonymised real situation that occurred in the last five years that sums up the hurt that can occur:

> Gemma was in her second year of university and had joined the Christian Union in her first year. She had been spotted as a likely leader of the future and, whilst many members didn't support women in leadership positions, she was nonetheless selected to go on the summer camp for future 'college representatives'. Whilst on this camp, she was drilled on the 'doctrinal basis of faith' that she was expected to sign up to and came back ready to start the term.
>
> During the holidays, Gemma's younger sister came out to her and the family. The family was not particularly religious and her coming out posed no serious threat to their relationship, but for Gemma it was a different story. In the first instance, she spoke at length with her sister, telling her that she still loved her but could not support her relationship. She spoke with her Christian Union mentors – themselves students with no theological training whatsoever – and they encouraged her in continuing to reject her sister's sinful choices.
>
> The problem is that Gemma ended up having an informal conversation with her college chaplain over breakfast, a man who her Christian Union friends had already denounced as un-orthodox. They got chatting

and in the course of the conversation, Gemma asked his prayers for her having to manage a sister who had chosen to turn away from God. This got a conversation started, and Gemma began to doubt whether she really needed to choose either Christian Union or her sister.

During the next few weeks, she became clearer in her own mind that there was nowhere near the contradiction that she had previously been told existed. She began to discuss this with her Christian Union friends, and one of them mentioned what she had said to her co-lead in the college. Leaders had been encouraged to bring any suggestion of unorthodoxy and so he immediately went to discuss it with the mentors.

One thing led to another, and she was hauled up in front of the leaders of the Christian Union to explain herself. It was made very simple for her – either you talk in orthodox (that is, anti-gay) terms, or you are excluded from the Christian Union. She chose her sister, regretting that she would lose her leadership position but entirely at peace with her decision.

The problem is that just losing her leadership position wasn't enough. Her friends in the Christian Union were informed – both directly and indirectly – that someone like this is not someone with whom a friendship is a good idea. So her so-called friends deserted her. Her life at university had been all about the Christian Union since her first week – they had promised an all-encompassing university experience in which she would be welcomed and nurtured. The small print wasn't really made part of the deal – but opposing, or even not fully affirming, the entirety of the 'doctrinal basis of faith' was enough to lose your place in that community entirely. You're on your own.

This is just the tip of the iceberg of the damage that such self-described Christian communities can do – Gemma wasn't even LGBTQI herself, but it was enough to oppose the powers and they would ensure you were dead to even your friends. The leadership sets the boundaries and outside of this you were not a Christian – just like the college chaplain. Orthodoxy is the preserve of the men in charge (and yes, they are usually men) and woe betide you if you take them on. This is all about control – of a narrative, of a movement, of individuals. Better to cast off the chaff than risk a loss of control. The problem is, that chaff is real people.

From a Christian perspective it is somewhat surprising that sex has become quite such a cornerstone of orthodoxy in these circles, although there has always been a temptation to control others' bodies throughout history, and the history of the Church is no exception. Sex provides a good nexus in this regard – controlling the body often helps those in power to control the mind, and throughout history women have primarily been the target of this kind of sex politics. The Church, to its great shame, has not been exempt from this kind of behaviour, and indeed has sponsored and furthered it. The man is to be obeyed, as we hear in the BCP marriage service; the woman is to be 'loved and cherished'.

It is easy to point fingers at the attitudes of the past, but it is no secret that the history of Christian culture has been one of patriarchy, that puts the (predominantly white) man at the centre of the picture. Man represents Christ at the altar; man is Christ to his bride the Church; man is the anatomical norm (despite the genetic evidence to the contrary); man is the head of the household. It is certainly possible to find some biblical backing for this, as we continue to see in churches that proclaim 'headship'; it is, nonetheless, also possible to find some biblical backing for slavery, if we go looking for it. This is the problem when a power-centred culture leads scriptural interpretation – we can always find what we want. Yet what the Bible itself calls for is for a journey to the periphery, and a valuing of the most vulnerable. The Church's opposition to LGBTQI people is just the most recent example of where the powerful have been privileged over the vulnerable.

The problem is that it is not a big jump – at least ideologically – from this kind of controlling environment to a cult that demands everything, defines everything, and ultimately can lead to immense damage because of it. In recent years we have begun to process the awful reality of sexual abuse in the Church and specifically that found in closed church groups right across the ecclesiological spectrum. Of note is the preponderance of powerful, white men at the helm of these cults, men who were either doing the abusing, or covering up or failing to believe those who came forward. It is abundantly clear that sex became not only a tool of abuse but also profoundly wrapped up in the abusive ideologies that flowed through these groups, and the evidence from the IICSA inquiry is worth revisiting at this point.

Bishop Martin Warner made reference to a '*dangerous spiritualising of sexual attraction under the guise of pastoral concern*', and the evidence from the inquiries into the most recent cases suggest that this spiritualising was one of many ways that sexual abuse was both excused and arguably encouraged by those at the top of these organisations, whether they were the ones committing the abuse or otherwise. It is clear that many of those committing abuse were themselves homosexual, yet rather than honest conversations about this, their sexual urges were 'spiritualised' and turned into a method of abuse for those who joined their all-encompassing cults. This is not a result of failing to follow a 'conservative' sexual ethic; it is a direct result of that very ethic coming into contact with the very heterosexualist patriarchy that so often precedes and fuels it. That so few seem willing to see the connection is a terrifying reality, producing a situation which continues to fan the flame of this kind of abusive ideology and practice. It is no coincidence that those whose vision of God is one that embraces repression end up leading and influencing movements whose core is deeply unhealthy in terms of sexuality and power.

At this point, it is worth considering once again the current teaching document of the Church of England, the rules of which continue to be applied to today's ordinands and clergy. *Issues in Human Sexuality*'s fifth chapter is entitled 'Homophiles in the Life and Fellowship of the Church', and towards the end of this chapter is found the current rulebook, which forbids any relational sexuality for LGBTQI ordinands or clergy. Yet the scene is set at the start of this chapter in a paragraph which perfectly illustrates the sociocultural assumptions and male heterosexualist power dynamic which infuses the development of these rules. We are told:[1]

> Homophile orientation and its expression in sexual activity do not constitute a parallel and alternative form of human sexuality as complete within the terms of the created order as the heterosexual. The convergence of Scripture, Tradition and reasoned reflection on experience, even including the newly sympathetic and perceptive thinking of our own day, make it impossible for the Church to come with integrity to any other conclusion. Heterosexuality and homosexuality are not equally congruous with the observed order of creation or with the insights of revelation as the Church engages with these in the light of her pastoral ministry.
>
> We are aware that some regard such a position as tantamount to a rejection of the homophile as a person. Personal identity, it is argued, is so fundamentally bound up with sexuality that to categorise the latter as

---

[1] *Issues in Human Sexuality* (London: Church House Publishing, 2003). It is interesting that the document is not currently easily available on the website of the Church of England, except in the section specifically relating to ordained ministry. Associated with this is an entirely disingenuous statement that reports 'there are no restrictions to ordination based on sexuality' (https://www.churchofengland.org/life-events/vocations/preparing-ordained-ministry/understanding-selection).

in some way imperfect is to treat the whole person as also essentially inferior. The argument is, however, false. Sexuality is a very important and influential element in our human make-up, but it is only one aspect of it. Our sexuality may vary from the norm in many ways, of which a homophile orientation is but one, without affecting our equal worth and dignity as human beings, which rests on the fact that all of us alike are made in the image of God. It is crucial to stress this point, because by equating the principle set out in the preceding paragraph with an inhuman rejection of the homophile person great harm has been done. Sexuality is given an inflated significance in human life; homophiles are wrongly made to feel devalued by the traditional teaching of the Church; and those who hold to that teaching are pressed to abandon it by implied accusations of cruelty and injustice.

There is much else within this document that could be analysed and rejected, yet these paragraphs are fundamental because they lay out so clearly the role that heterosexualism plays within the Church of England. This is not, we must remind ourselves, a historical document – this is the living document that continues to influence the lives of clergy in the Church of England, and is used to forbid them from entering or continuing ministry. It is fascinating that *Issues* immediately states – with a broad but shallow flourish towards the Anglican three-legged stool – that homosexuality is fundamentally inferior to heterosexuality, and it is this starting point that feeds the entirety of the rest of this chapter. It is interesting that even in this teaching document, the underlying premise of this book is accepted, yet it does not appear that the bishops who accepted this report followed this premise to anything like its conclusion.

This much can be seen in the paragraph which follows this assertion. It is very easy for heterosexuals to describe sexuality as having an 'inflated significance in human life', but what this translates into is a silencing of the reality of non-heterosexual sexuality, as though it is a nuisance that is 'overstated' in the lives of those who experience it. Of course, for heterosexuals their sexuality is the norm – there is nothing special about it by its nature because it is what is expected. Blithe statements about all being made in the image of God do nothing to improve matters – it brings to mind the Cambridge college chapel where the 'conservative' Dean was so embarrassed about there being a group of LGBTQI people there to celebrate LGBT history month that he started the service by saying 'I would like to particularly welcome ... everyone ... to this service'.

To ignore the importance of sexuality to the heterosexual and homosexual alike is a nonsense, and it is a mark of seriously low levels of introspection not to recognise that it is only to heterosexuals that homosexual sexuality is so foreign. Sexuality, and most particularly relational sexuality, is not an optional extra – it is fundamental to an individual's sense of self and wellbeing, and indeed their way of interacting with the world, as we have seen in previous chapters. The argument made here is one that once again attempts to separate the 'act' from the 'identity' – although in this case, it is almost more pernicious, in attempting to slice out sexuality from the wider web of personality and identity as if it is possible to do so. The document ends by stating 'if we are faithful to our Lord then disagreement over the proper expression of homosexual love will never become rejection of the homosexual person'. This is so – yet even a basic level of serious analysis would show that the preceding paragraphs do just this by creating false dichotomies and ultimately a denial of the whole human person, LGBTQI or otherwise.

The problem is not only the faulty logic and poor argument found in *Issues in Human Sexuality* – it is that this document continues to be the source of alleged wisdom and ultimately discipline on this topic. It is certain that several, or indeed many, bishops would reject the arguments made in this document –in content, form, and aetiology – yet these same bishops nonetheless continue to enforce the rules that have been made based on these arguments. This is dishonest and ultimately harmful, not least because any rule that is enforced needs to be justified with more than a vague appeal to authority. Indeed, Article 32 of the 39 Articles is quite clear that 'it is lawful for [bishops, priests and deacons], as for all other Christian men [sic], to marry at their own discretion, as they shall judge the same to serve better to godliness.' An appeal to the Articles might appear to be a cheap endeavour, yet these articles form a part of the historic formularies of the Church of England which are directly referred to in the Declaration of Assent made at ordination and appointments because they embody something of the Church of England's self-understanding. For a document to appear to overrule this freedom requires that document to be a work of serious logic and theology. *Issues in Human Sexuality* does not fit that bill.

Yet it is not only within *Issues* that the problems arise. The recent Formation Criteria for Ordained Ministry in the Church of England[2] (in place until 2021) had a section entitled 'Relationships' with a number of different 'dispositions, understanding and skills' that clergy are expected to develop during their training. The most concerning and yet seemingly innocuous statement found within this document stated that ordinands should 'relate empathetically to those with whom they differ' in matters of 'sexual morality'. At first glance this seems uncontroversial, yet we find here, once again, a key example of heterosexualism. That 'sexual morality' is code for homosexuality is blindingly obvious, given the associated mention of *Issues*, and this calls into question the appropriateness of asking LGBTQI people to 'relate empathetically' to those who believe they are intrinsically

---

2 Recently this specific document has been replaced for ordinands and potential ordinands in the Church of England. However, the Church of England continues to state that 'All candidates for ordination must affirm they are willing to live within the Bishops' guidelines on *Issues in Human Sexuality*': https://www.churchofengland.org/life-events/vocations/preparing-ordained-ministry/understanding-selection.

disordered and should accept a sexual morality built on a flimsy document that ultimately forbids them from any relational sexual expression. 'Empathy' is a very strange word to use – the Merriam-Webster dictionary definition describes it as:[3]

> The action of understanding, being aware of, being sensitive to, and vicariously experiencing the feelings, thoughts, and experience of another of either the past or present without having the feelings, thoughts, and experience fully communicated in an objectively explicit manner.

Asking LGBTQI ordinands to empathise in this manner – to deliberately attempt to vicariously experience the feelings, thoughts and experience of another - with those who deny this aspect of their sense of self is nothing short of an act of emotional violence. It is unthinkable that we would ask other minority groups in society to empathise in this way – it is simply another example of the blind-spot that so consistently applies to LGBTQI people and their experience.

At heart, then, there is a structural problem in the way the Church of England relates to LGBTQI people – a structural problem shared by many other churches that embody it in similar and related ways. The Church, by its nature, is driven by a narrative of male heterosexuality, and unless and until this is replaced with a narrative of humanity then the ongoing structural problems will remain. LGBTQI people – and their bodies – are frequently described in the narrative as part of the problem, rather than part of the solution. LGBTQI people find themselves, therefore, in a deeply pernicious environment, where false equivalences are made between the genuine oppression of LGBTQI people and theological disagreement with 'conservatives', and where they are frequently expected to model perfect behaviour in the face of abuse. LGBTQI

---

[3] https://www.merriam-webster.com/dictionary/empathy.

people are told that they are making too big a deal out of their 'issues' and that there are more urgent or important things to worry about than their 'obsession' with sexuality. They are told to 'bide their time' and frequently told to 'calm down', as if this is an abstract conversation. Their vocation is questioned and they face the end of their ministry if they make a formal and legal commitment to someone of the same sex.

Meanwhile, their identity is fair game for 'discussion', their commitment to scripture is consistently questioned, their integrity is dismissed, their arguments are wilfully misrepresented, their experiences are discounted or trivialised, they are described as an 'ideology' and they are continually spoken *about* not *with*, because the heart of the Church establishment still sees them as 'the other' rather than as integrated, beloved, children of God. It is in this kind of environment that LGBTQI people are successfully gas-lighted, belittled, delegitimised and scapegoated. It is also in this environment that those with the power either do nothing on their behalf – either uninterested or behaving like bystanders paralysed by fear – or actively persecute them. This is what structural violence looks like, however 'gently' or 'generously' it is expressed.

LGBTQI people are deeply vulnerable in the Church: spiritually, reputationally, financially, psychologically. They appear to have very few allies amongst the powerful who are willing to take a stand, and their continued vulnerability highlights the deranged power dynamics of the contemporary church. Their experience points towards a much wider problem that desperately needs fixing – a structural imbalance that requires determined, conscious and active work to address. At present, there is far too little of this in evidence. Ultimately, a church that has an unhealthy relationship with power is a church that is safe for nobody, and a church which will ultimately trample the most vulnerable underfoot. It is for this reason that the lives and experience of LGBTQI people must be taken seriously and seen not as an irritation or an aberration but as a gift to a sick church. The Church needs LGBTQI people as much as they need it, and it is only when they are truly treated as equal, beloved, holy children of God that the Church will ever thrive. It is in the vulnerable that the face of God is seen, not the powerful; it is the vulnerable and oppressed who find their home in the heart of God. It is with Mary that they sing:

> 'My soul magnifies the Lord,
> and my spirit rejoices in God my Saviour,
> for he has looked with favour on the lowliness of his servant.
> Surely, from now on all generations will call me blessed;
> for the Mighty One has done great things for me,
> and holy is his name.
> His mercy is for those who fear him
> from generation to generation.
> He has shown strength with his arm;
> he has scattered the proud in the thoughts of their hearts.
> He has brought down the powerful from their thrones,
> and lifted up the lowly;
> he has filled the hungry with good things,
> and sent the rich away empty.
> He has helped his servant Israel,
> in remembrance of his mercy,
> according to the promise he made to our ancestors,
> to Abraham and to his descendants forever.'
>
> (Luke 1:46-55)

9

INCLUSION OR EXCLUSION

The chapters in this section have focused on what the current repressive atmosphere and actions have done to the life of the Church and its people. We have seen the damage that is done by the false separation of sexuality and self; we have seen the way that culture can be poisoned by repression, and how this interacts with and ultimately encourages a culture of power and control. Whilst we have focussed on the lives of LGBTQI people, we have seen the way that this issue reveals much about the wider functioning of the Church, and how LGBTQI people have often borne the brunt of other fights, in which they become nothing more than pawns in a bigger game. We have seen how the LGBTQI narrative has so often been shut down, and LGBTQI people have been described as a 'problem' for the rest of the Church. Ultimately, we have seen the loss of so much potential – the loss of healthy relationships, the loss of good people, and the failure of the Church to fully embody its mission and ministry. Far from being a problem, LGBTQI people – their narratives and their lives – are part of the solution to a culture and an attitude that has overshadowed the Church for too long, yet the Church continues to either refuse to acknowledge this, or is unable to do so.

At this point it is important to state something that is entirely obvious – we might be wrong. It may indeed be the case that God does condemn any relational sexuality outside of a heterosexual marriage, and that the readings of scripture that lead to this view might indeed be right. Human experience and human discovery may indeed go against this, but that may present no problem for God – we may have much more to discover and we may find that what we currently believe to be true is false or superseded by other evidence. It is somewhat hard to imagine any good reason for this and it doesn't appear to fit with the revelatory history of God and God's purposes, but we should always be open to this possibility. Contingency is key to the argument of this book, and it is when contingency is shelved that the problems we have encountered are most keenly seen.

Yet this is not the same as saying that the perceived effects on the culture of the Church that we have described are false. Indeed, even if relational sexuality is forbidden by God's will to LGBTQI people, that does not make the evidenced effects of repression any less real. If God forbids LGBTQI relational sexuality, then the Church needs to grapple with the evidenced consequences rather than simply continue the way we are. It is not good enough to say that because the Bible is clear, then it is acceptable to erase the lives and experience of LGBTQI people as we currently do, nor to ignore the huge cultural problems that have been highlighted by the plight of LGBQTI Christians. At the very least these things need to be faced head on, recognised and engaged with. Business as usual is not acceptable given what we know.

Unfortunately, this does not seem to be the case. It is clear that, for a large number of churches that oppose LGBTQI sexual expression, there is a determination to continue the erasure in the refusal to discuss LGBTQI people on their terms, with a preference for terms such as 'same-sex attracted', 'lifestyle choice' and abstract discussions on 'the issue'. This has to change, and those who claim to want a more inclusive and welcoming environment for LGBQTI people despite a 'conservative' position on sexual expression need to make clear and obvious attempts to bring about this change. There is great fury elicited when such churches are described as homophobic, yet such a label is entirely appropriate if this kind of erasure continues (and when such churches do not openly and vocally support the civil rights of LGBTQI people). The arguments made in this book are pertinent to those of any theological persuasion, and the evidence needs to be taken seriously. It is no longer acceptable to pretend there is no problem, or that the Bible requires the silencing of the LGBTQI voice. LGBTQI people exist and must be met on their own terms. Their sexual expression may be something that 'conservatives' wish to forbid, but to deny their existence, or to suggest that heteronormativity as a culture is entirely exclusive of other sexualities is simply wrong.

Indeed, it is all part of a culture war that has been whipped up by 'conservatives' in order to point the finger of blame at those who don't fit the norm. These aberrant people are the problem, the argument goes, and their 'lifestyles' cannot possibly fit within the Christian church. The problem with this position is that its starting point is culture rather than God: it assumes that the Church of God must, by its nature, be monocultural, and thus must require adherence, and even loyalty, to one, particular, cultural way of 'being church'. This is nonsense, not least because of the biblical record, and the record of Christian history. The Epistles are not letters to a monoculture – they are letters to specific, enculturated, different churches in different places, all of which are centred on Christ, the fundamentals of the faith, the preaching of the Word and the sacraments, yet each within their own context. That there are some non-negotiables is certainly evident, and that there is a common thread throughout is also clear – but that is not the same as replacing faith with cultural adherence.

Christianity as a faith is ultimately belief in the incarnation, life, death and resurrection of Jesus Christ, the saviour of the world, and a recognition that these events and this belief change everything. Culture is entirely secondary to that, and when culture becomes more important than the faith, then we end up in significant trouble – we need only think of the prosperity Gospel or the Nazified church to see where this kind of thinking gets us. That is not to say that Christianity does not make demands on culture – quite the opposite. Christianity must be the refining fire in which culture is held, that leads to the casting out of those things that are antithetical to the Kingdom. But we must be very careful when we call everything about particular cultures ungodly – this carries resonances of the imperialist past, in which white Christianity was thought to be the only Christianity, leading to significant evil. There is an ongoing dialogue about syncretism which we must pay attention to, but it is nonetheless not at all clear that a heterosexualist culture is required by God. Casting out LGBTQI people and the cultures that they have developed – very often cultures of resistance that chime convincingly with Christian themes – because of an opposition to sexual expression seems entirely inappropriate.

Catastrophising arguments are, however, frequently made by those who oppose LGBTQI sexual expression. One of the key arguments made against equal marriage – a topic we turn to in the next chapter – was that because it was a 'redefinition' of marriage by the state, then it would devalue current heterosexual marriages. This argument is somewhat bizarre, as in the same breath many 'conservatives' would argue that same-sex marriage is impossible 'by definition', so it is not at all clear how something can be both impossible but also devastating to the decades-long marriages of heterosexuals. Nonetheless, this was a frequent argument put forward, and is a clear example of the fear tactics employed by those who themselves do genuinely appear to fear the outcomes of societal change. The problem for these arguments is that they are demonstrably false. We now have the evidence of what happens in societies where same-sex marriages are introduced, and the reality is that no huge breakdown in society has occurred and heterosexual marriages have not been destabilised *en masse*.[1] In fact, in many ways the support of LGBTQI people has added to social cohesion rather than reduced it, and the celebration of Pride, for example, has not led to any kind of social breakdown.

This is, in many ways, fundamentally unacceptable to a 'conservative' mindset, yet we have seen time and time again in society how movements for progressive change have not led to the dire outcomes predicted. The list of such 'progressive' movements is long – women's suffrage, civil rights for black and minority ethnic people, the rights of the disabled, to mention a few. Each time moves have been made to liberate groups of people, fears have been raised by factions within society that any such moves would lead to the breakdown of the family and society as a whole. On no occasion has this been the case.

It is worth for one moment focusing on the 'fetishisation' of the family that has occurred throughout western society, and most particularly in church cultures, over the past two centuries. There is not the space here to fully investigate the history, but it is abundantly clear that the two live at home parent family with several smiling children has not been the norm throughout Christian history.[2] Yet in recent years, this has been seen as the Christian norm, with anything outside of it seen as aberrant and threatening. Not only does this affect LGBTQI people, but it also affects single parents and many others for whom this living situation is not their lived experience. The writings of Paul and indeed through much of the patristic period by no means point towards

---

[1]   Once again, it is easy to pick and choose studies, but it is much better to get a view of the literature from reviews and similar. A good place to start if readers wish to explore the wider landscape might be Eskridge Jr, W. N., and Spedale, D. R., *Gay Marriage: For Better or for Worse?* (Oxford: Oxford University Press, 2006) and Issenberg, S., *The Engagement* (New York: Knopf Doubleday, 2021).

[2]   A helpful and interesting guide would be Thatcher, A. (ed.), *The Oxford Handbook of Theology, Sexuality, and Gender* (Oxford: Oxford University Press, 2014), which also touches on several of the wider topics in this book.

this particular manifestation of Christian life as the only acceptable monoculture, yet far too often this is held up as the 'Christian' way as opposed to other ways of living. This does great damage not only to those individuals who do not or cannot live like this, but also to the self-understanding of the Church.

The moment that a church exists as a monoculture, then a host of undesirable consequences follow. In the first instance, it automatically becomes a place of exclusion, inadvertently or otherwise. If a church's website shows their large leadership team as a set of white, middle class, heterosexual couples, then that is immediately a crisis in representation and is likely to be off-putting to large swathes of society, however many welcoming smiles that team's pictures contain. This will have a huge impact on the mission possibilities in such a parish, and whilst it may attract other white, middle class, heterosexual couples, it is unlikely to attract those who don't fit into this paradigm. Even if others walk through the door, if the Church culture itself is white, middle class and heterosexual, then it is unlikely they will stay, or if they do, that they will put themselves forward for leadership roles. This is the second problem with monocultures – they are likely to remain so. One of the key – indeed foundational – truths about the Church is that it is genuinely a place for everyone, and does not discriminate on the basis of any external characteristic. A church that embodies a monoculture does discriminate – albeit unconsciously. Yet given we know this is the case, there is no excuse to discriminate, consciously or unconsciously.

Whilst the Church has, in recent years, begun to get to grips with these issues of representation and monoculture, it has been noticeably silent in its willingness to even recognise, let alone celebrate, the contribution of different LGBTQI cultures. This is by no means the case across the board – many churches do attend Pride marches and will make active attempts to visibly include LGBTQI people, including at leadership level.[3] That said, the Church of England continues to make it very challenging for LGBTQI people to become ordained because of its refusal to move forward from the rules we have previously considered, that developed out of *Issues* and ultimately forbid sexual expression of any kind.

Yet one very clear missing element is any recognition that LGBTQI cultures might have something to teach the Church, rather than the other way around. Again, this is not a new phenomenon, but it is one that appears to have stuck in this sphere. LGBTQI people are still referred to as promiscuous, subversive, dangerous, and this is often linked back to 'gay culture' which is feared rather than engaged with. It may indeed be outside the comfort zone of many senior leaders in the Church of England, not least because those who are more senior and thus older may have particular stereotypes of 'gay culture' that continue to be influenced by fears of AIDS and other prejudiced hangovers. Yet not only are these views unwarranted and ignorant in the first place, views that themselves led to further oppression and othering of LGBTQI people, but they also blind church leaders to the potential and life-giving, raw and often explosive joy that LGBTQI cultures embody – joy that is born out of hardship and oppression, indeed joy that might easily speak with the words of the Psalms. We shall consider the gifts of LGBTQI people in our final chapter, yet it is worth noting here that the deliberate silencing of LGBTQI cultures out of fear not only

---

[3] Such engagements are invariably met with protest: a prime example would be the flying of the Rainbow Flag at Ely Cathedral in 2018, which was met with outrage from a former Anglican priest, Gavin Ashenden, who stated, 'the Dean is choosing the Leftist values of so-called 'breadth and diversity' (values found nowhere in the Christian Gospels) and wants to make reparation for the fact that Christians have been insufficiently supportive of non-monogamous and heterosexual sexual adventure (code word 'inclusivity'- another term found nowhere in the teaching of Jesus.)', alleging that the Dean of Ely had 'adopted the secular values of a culture that has set its face against Christianity, and is waging a war against Judaeo-Christian culture'. Such hyperbole is not uncommon (https://premierchristian.news/en/news/article/ely-cathedral-flying-rainbow-flag-is-blasphemy-priest-says).

does further damage to LGBTQI Christians' integrated sense of self, but also leaves churches much the poorer as well.

We have previously discussed the oft-trumpeted importance of being 'counter-cultural' in Christian witness. The virtue associated with counter-cultural positioning is often highlighted when Christians talk about sexuality in the twenty-first century world – the argument being that Christians are called to stay true against the machinations of the world, an idea primarily based on the writing of St Paul (Romans 12:2):

> Do not be conformed to this world, but be transformed by the renewing of your minds, so that you may discern what is the will of God—what is good and acceptable and perfect.

The principle itself is not problematic, but its implementation often is. It is interesting that those who wheel out the term do not refer to the remainder of this chapter in Romans, which speaks of the importance of the variety of members of the body of Christ ('so we, who are many, are one body in Christ, and individually we are members of one another' (v.6)), and of the importance of loving 'one another with mutual affection; outdo one another in showing honour' (v.11). Indeed, Romans 12 is perhaps a foundational text for reimagining the Christian culture away from its current monoculture.

The issue with the kind of simplistic use of verse 12 to oppose LGBTQI people is that, like we have seen throughout Chapters 2 and 3, biblical interpretation is not quite as simple as that. The world has compromised on LGBTQI issues, we are told, and the Church must stand tall and firm against this destruction of the moral order. The problem is that this is a deeply imperialist mindset in the first instance – the world may well be gentler and more hospitable towards LGBTQI people in the west (in the main), but that is by no means true across the world. It is certainly counter-cultural in some UK settings to oppose LGBTQI inclusion, but it is most certainly not in countries where you can be put to death for simply being homosexual. Across the Anglican Communion, there are a number of countries where church leaders have actively sponsored governments' attempts to criminalise LGBTQI people; it is extremely hard to describe this as anything other than entirely concordant with the dominant culture.

The reality is that this verse does not sanction being counter-cultural for its own sake, as any serious interpreter of Paul's letters would understand. Instead, it is arguable that the thesis of this book is found in this verse as its interpretative key – the 'renewing of your minds', that allows discernment of the things of the world – those things that are in opposition to God, and not necessarily 'of the world' in terms of any particular culture. It is foolishness to consider any particular culture fully good or fully bad – indeed, that is one of the key messages of the Bible. God's Kingdom is good, and yet there are many things 'of the world' that oppose it – we are called to seek and ask for the Spirit's aid in discerning which things are of God and which are not. A lazy, sweeping statement about the world supporting LGBTQI rights is nothing more than that – a lazy, sweeping statement. It says nothing whatsoever about the rightness or wrongness of this when viewed through the lens of the Kingdom of God.

We have already noted that St Paul (and the writers of the other epistles) is writing to a whole host of different churches found in their very different contexts and with their very different challenges. However, there is something else very much worth noting about St Paul's letters – they are written to, and not about, these different churches. St Paul's theology, then, is contextual by its nature – it is a theology that seeks to respond to particular contexts and problems, yet with an overarching theological narrative that develops as time passes. It is also a theology that meets people where they are and does not seek to erase or airbrush their existence. There are most certainly some reprimands in the epistles – one need only think of the troublesome and elitist Church of Corinth – but Paul does not write promoting a particular church culture but rather to spread the good news into each place. Rather than writing in the abstract, he speaks to the situation found in specific places, and it is fascinating that this great foundational Christian theologian's writing comes to us not as abstract theory, but as applied and lived particularities. Paul is not a theologian who airbrushed out of existence those for whom his abstractions did not fit; instead, he grapples with each community, and its culture, and seeks to make it part of the Kingdom.

This is another example of where the Bible, through its own narrative and structure, can call attention to where we fall short in our interpretation and ultimately in our vocation as Christians. Discernment is a key part of the life of the Christian, and in the case of LGBTQI people, this discernment means genuinely listening to – and respecting the integrity of – LGBTQI people themselves. Casting unfounded and prejudiced aspersions on them, or describing them or their lives in hyperbolic and negative ways, is not the way of Christ and does not afford them the dignity they deserve, whatever one thinks of their sexual preferences or sexuality.

Of course, discrimination against LGBTQI people is sometimes quite deliberate, but much of the time it is a much murkier picture, with conscious and unconscious elements contributing to a complex web of prejudice. In this section of the book, we have seen the role of an unhealthy culture in this, but it is not always plain to those who are caught up in this web that they are being affected by it. It is easy to point the finger at LGBTQI people and tell them that they cannot think or speak about these issues without bias, but the same is true of anyone. Questions of personal identity, sexuality and similar, are questions about which it is not possible to be entirely objective, and questions for which it is impossible to truly empathise with someone in a different position than oneself. We can, of course, attempt to do so, but it is introspection and reflection that offer the best hope of doing so, together with a fundamental acceptance that we cannot ever truly be objective.

Our inability to extricate ourselves from our culture is also a major reason for constantly ensuring that we are viewing our situations or those of others in the light of the gospel rather than the other way around. The problem is that our current church culture remains one of patriarchy and heterosexualism, and we frequently end up reading the gospel in the light of our culture. It is extremely difficult to do otherwise, and this is nothing new – for years, the Church read (and in many ways continues to read) the gospel in the light of patriarchy, bringing prejudice and preconceptions to the interpretative lens and thus finding that for which they sought, either consciously or unconsciously. These kinds of readings turn the gospel into an unwitting tool of culture, rather than the other way around, yet it is inevitable that every reading of the Bible will ultimately carry some of this baggage. It is for this reason that it is so important to make use of the corrective that multiple cultural interpretations of the Bible offer; to believe that some cultures, backgrounds or experiences have nothing to offer is to almost ensure that a blind spot is inserted into our understanding.

When all the evidence is considered, it is quite clear that the current attitude of the Church to LGBTQI people is one that wreaks significant damage, not just to LGBTQI people, but to the wider church as well. Ultimately, this is a huge risk for the ministry and mission of the Church – a risk whose consequences we have already seen, whether it is the tragic deaths of those unable to cope with prejudice, or the rejection of the Church and its crucial Gospel message by those who see it as an agent of moral evil. It remains baffling that those who favour a 'conservative' position do not see – and often do not care – how wider society sees the Church, or how its position on LGBTQI people is a major barrier not only to growth, but to being listened to at all. Church leaders spend much time and energy talking about the importance of anti-racism or opposing misogyny, yet whilst we continue to actively discriminate against LGBTQI people – using specific opt-outs from the Equality Act (2010) in the UK – our ability to speak on these topics with anything like a moral voice is utterly compromised. Our structural homophobia is a catastrophe for our mission, and particularly for young people – although increasingly for those of all ages – our position on LGBTQI people is either met with utter bewilderment, or vehement opposition.

We have already considered the inadequacy of the arguments that state the Church must be 'counter-cultural' at all costs, and it is quite simply not good enough to reject the views of 'the world' in this way. For far too long, the Church has satisfied itself with these arguments, with a mistaken belief that the world hating it is, even, further justification for its position. The Church need not feel the need to oblige the world by changing its views, we are told, without a single thought apparently being given as to why the world's view might have changed in the first place. It is high time for this to end. The Church must, of course, not change its doctrine solely because the world has changed its view – but to refuse to even engage with why this might have happened, with all the evidence on human flourishing pointing in one direction, is absurd.

Whereas previously the Church's opposition to the flourishing of LGBTQI people within its ranks only really affected those within the institution, this is no longer the case. The loud appeals by the Church of England against the introduction of Civil Partnerships and then Equal Marriage (discussed in the next chapter) woke society up to how far the Church has drifted from wider society on this topic, and even those people who would normally remain totally uninterested or uninformed about its position have become aware of its opposition. The Church didn't merely attempt to stop such marriages taking place in church, but rather launched an active opposition to the law more generally, hugely overreaching their authority (and overestimating their support) in an attempt to control the secular realm. Whether this was borne out of a ludicrous lack of introspection or was simply the work of overexcited bishops is not clear, but the Church of England came bounding onto the scene, making it clear that they were fundamentally opposed to the freedom of LGBTQI people to marry even in civil ceremonies. This was a huge misjudgement and the Church is often seen to be on the side of the oppressor and not the oppressed in modern Britain.

The seriousness of this has quite simply not sunk in. The Church's position on LGBTQI people barely even gets a mention when mission is being discussed, and far more is said about the alleged virtue of 'not following the world' than is ever said about the Church's mission to (and with) LGBTQI people themselves. For apologists, it is extremely challenging to point to serious reasons why belonging to the Church of England would be of benefit to LGBTQI people in happy and functional relationships. There are arguments to be made, of course, but it is most certainly understandable when LGBTQI people avoid the Church like the plague. It is noticeable that even the mention of Christianity amongst young people is frequently accompanied by disgust over the Church's treatment of LGBTQI people. To be frank, a Christian is viewed as a homophobe and transphobe until proven otherwise. This is a shocking position for the Church to find itself in and is testament to the power of foolish words and closed ears in the life of the Church.

Yet it is not only LGBTQI people who will not come near the Church. As society has opened up and recognised the existence of, and beauty of, LGBTQI lives, more and more families have experience of LGBTQI children, grandchildren, nieces and nephews, and this means that the Church's abstractions become real to more and more people within and without the institution. Given the flimsiness of the reasons for continuing opposition to LGBTQI relational sexuality, it remains quite inexplicable that those in authority in the Church have not made any serious effort to embrace LGBQTI people as children of God beyond the occasional warm words. There are LGBTQI people desperate to make commitments to each other in front of God, and to seek to live lives serving the Church. It is extraordinary that the Church makes it so difficult for them.

Those within the Church, however, appear keen to suggest that LGBTQI people are making too much out of what is, in fact, a 'relatively minor issue'. LGBTQI people should be less angry, they are told, and should love the Church more – despite that church behaving like an abusive parent. Those who have no LGBTQI relatives and are strong members of the institution may indeed feel that the emphasis placed on LGBTQI inclusion is far too much, but it is very easy to say this when it does not affect you, your children or your grandchildren. Meanwhile, the Church of England frequently talks about inclusivity without even mentioning LGBTQI people, unwittingly – and sometimes quite deliberately – playing into a narrative that pits different disadvantaged groups against each other and ignores the key insights that models of intersectionality have provided in recent years. Even on those occasions that the Church has offered an apology for past homophobia, this is too frequently mealy-mouthed. Warm words are cheap, like those from the meeting of the Primates of the Anglican Communion in 2016, in which it is noticeable that the word gay was not even mentioned:[4]

> The Primates condemned homophobic prejudice and violence and resolved to work together to offer pastoral care and loving service irrespective of sexual orientation. This conviction arises out of our discipleship of Jesus Christ. The Primates reaffirmed their rejection of criminal sanctions against same-sex attracted people.

These words have not been followed up by any serious

---

[4] https://www.anglicannews.org/features/2016/01/communique-from-the-primates-meeting-2016.aspx.

action, and in 2021 the Archbishop of Nigeria stated:[5]

> 'The deadly "virus" of homosexuality has infiltrated the Anglican Church of North America. This is likened to a yeast that should be urgently and radically expunged and excised lest it affects the whole dough.'

Whilst it is true that the Archbishop of Canterbury eventually spoke out, it is noticeable that it was the language and not the sentiment that he opposed:[6]

> 'I completely disagree with and condemn this language. It is unacceptable. It dehumanises those human beings of whom the statement speaks.'

This is not a strong example of the condemnation of

5   https://www.episcopalnewsservice.org/2021/03/05/archbishop-of-canterbury-condemns-nigerian-primates-anti-gay-language/

6   https://www.archbishopofcanterbury.org/news/news-and-statements/statement-archbishop-canterbury-regarding-comments-primate-nigeria. Earlier chapters have discussed the dynamics of the Anglican Communion and highlighted the 2021 'anti-LGBTQ Bill' in Ghana. On this occasion, there was once again a significant period during which no English bishop spoke out, eventually followed by a statement from the link diocese of Portsmouth and a statement from the Archbishop of Canterbury (albeit a statement that appeared to be qualified at a later date). The Archbishop's initial statement referred back to the Communique of 2016 and appeared to make a link between the importance of opposition to homophobia and the opposition to same-sex marriage, whilst his later statement opined that 'cultural, social and historical contexts must also be considered and understood' in relation to LGBTQI people (https://www.archbishopofcanterbury.org/news/news-and-statements/archbishop-canterburys-statement-following-meeting-archbishop-bishops-and). It is worth noting, of course, that society and culture are often used as the bogeymen and focuses of opposition in 'conservative' discourse on sexuality in the UK, yet here – when it suits – they appear to be seen in a rather more convenient light. Whilst this all may have been targeted at the Ghanaian bishops, it once again sent a lukewarm signal to LGBTQI people in the UK – amongst them Ghanaians – and in Ghana itself, and utilised the language of 'same-sex attraction' which even the virulently prejudicial Bill in Ghana did not do (https://www.archbishopofcanterbury.org/news/news-and-statements/archbishop-canterburys-statement-ghanas-anti-lgbtq-bill). It is worth bearing in mind that the Bill called for imprisonment of LGBTQI people and their supporters, amongst other drastic measures.

homophobic prejudice. Meanwhile, it is those churches that marry LGBTQI people that are excluded from some decision-making parts of the Anglican Communion whilst the Primate of Nigeria – himself already heavily involved in the leadership of the arguably schismatic GAFCON group – faces no consequences except a censure over the use of language. It is entirely understandable that LGBTQI people feel gaslit, ignored, devalued, debased and ultimately hated. It is inexplicable that those in authority cannot understand this, and instead frequently tell LGBTQI people to calm down and show more restraint. This is a case-study in victimising the victim, and is a prime example of how damaged the ministry of the Church has been left due to the current state of affairs.

That all said, this is not a book that is arguing for an end to the Church, and nor is it making the argument that all is lost. We are most certainly facing serious problems and the appalling record of the Church in its relationship with and to LGBTQI people is plain for all to see. This section has highlighted where things have gone wrong and shone a light into some of the darkest corners of the sorry state of Christ's own body, yet it has not done so for its own sake, but to argue for a radical rethinking of the Church's life and work. There is much work to be done, but the Church continues to be fed by people of all walks of life who are ready to enter the vineyard. As we move into the next Section, we will start to chart out what the future might look like, in a church that regards the world with curiosity and openness, and listens to those who are different, treating them as the family that they truly are.

The Church of England – and churches like it – are worth saving because they proclaim the saving Gospel of Jesus Christ. It is not humankind that will save the Church – it is Jesus Christ, the incarnate, risen saviour. Those who remain in the Church, working for justice, do so because they see the Lord at work, even when the darkest night seems to be never-ending. This book seeks to chart a way to that future, which is not antithetical to the Gospel, but is instead seeped in the narrative of the Bible, our tradition, our reason, our experience and our Christian journey. All is not lost, and one day LGBTQI people will finally be seen as the gift that they are, rather than as a problem to be solved. One day, LGBTQI people will be included by the Church in a way they are already included by God. For with Him, nothing is impossible.

> Let justice roll down like waters,
> and righteousness like an ever-flowing stream.
>
> (Amos 5:24)

PART III

10

SEX AND MARRIAGE

The preceding chapters in this book have painted something of a bleak picture.

It is important to be utterly blunt about the rejection and even hate that LGBTQI people have faced from the Church, including the Church of England. The question of whether the Church is homophobic is something often discussed and denied by church folk, but even brief conversations with LGBTQI people will make it abundantly clear that the answer is a resounding 'yes'. Individual Christians may not themselves be anti-LGBTQI, but at the structural level – in which we all participate – there is no denying that the Church's overall attitude and behaviour towards LGBTQI people is anything but life-enhancing. This is where we are, and as is the case when relating to other oppressed groups both now and throughout history, it is important for us to be clear about the reality of the current situation in order to move forward. The point is not to encourage self-flagellation or, inadvertently, to encourage even further defensiveness on the part of the Church. It is also not to encourage vitriol or rage against the Church, which – after all – is Christ's. It is rather to raise a clarion call for action, and to call the Church back to its sacred calling. A church that oppresses any of the children of God has lost some of its very essence and needs corrective therapy.

In this final section, we will start to sketch out what a true *aggiornamento* through *ressourcement* might look like in relation to LGBTQI people.[1] Any such change is going to be by its very nature contingent – it is in some respects a dive into an unknown sea, yet at the same time, it is a future that is governed and mapped out by the fundamentals of the past. It is truly radical – of the root – because it is a future that places Christ at its centre and the Christian way at its heart. The externals may indeed look different, but the core itself remains the Christian anthropology of the ages. This is no rudderless ship, in which all our previous understanding is jettisoned, yet it is a journey during which we must constantly remain open to the refining fires of scripture, tradition, reason and experience. There is much still to learn, and there is much in which to be guided by the Holy Spirit. It is this tension between the pioneering spirit and the anchor of faith that has characterised all Spirit-led movements for change in the Church.

Those who have been campaigning for LGBTQI equality in the Church have nonetheless spent many years being faced with brick walls and soothed by false promises. That we are still where we are – almost ten years on from the debates on same-sex marriage in the secular world – is a tragedy. It is a tragedy for the LGBTQI people who have been so badly hurt by the Church; it is a tragedy for our mission and for those so repulsed by our positioning that they have rejected the Church and the Lord; it is a tragedy for the health of the Church. Such a tragedy must grieve the heart of God. Despite this, LGBTQI people remain faithful to God, and believe that He will remain faithful to His promises. The time is now ripe for change to come, and it will be in the daily alertness to the work and movement of the Spirit that we will begin to discern the fruits of this change.

We have met the doom-mongers in the previous chapter – those who decry any change as intrinsically bad – and

---

[1] These terms were introduced in Chapter 3 and refer to defining concepts of the Second Vatican Council, formulated by Pope Saint John XXIII.

have roundly rejected their hypothesis. In general, however, any proposed change in the practice of the Church remains mired in fear and paralysed by intense caution, even amongst those who believe current church teaching to be quite wrong. Yet we must be clear that the warm words of previous years are no longer enough – indeed, they are little short of insulting. To describe oneself as supportive without making any effort to bring about meaningful change is simply disingenuous, and the reality is that the Church of England – like other churches in the Anglican Communion and more widely – is going to need to stop kicking the can down the road at some point. There is no time like the present; it is hard to understand how, presented with the litany just touched on in this book, any cogent argument could be made for yet more dither and delay.

To be blunt, a change in attitude is inextricably linked with a change in action. Being nicer to LGBTQI people, or saying you wish you could bless them, is ultimately meaningless if you are in a position to effect change – however small, and however limited your individual action might be. Words without actions may have been enough at the start of this campaign for human dignity but given the number of words and the total absence of any meaningful action, words without actions are little more than worthless. We shall think about the practical workings-out of this further in the concluding chapters of this book, but for now it is important to be clear that unless and until LGBTQI people have access to the sacraments, rites, and public ministry of the Church in the way that heterosexuals currently do, then there is no equality – and with it, a continued lack of human dignity afforded. It is for this reason that we need to turn to the debate on marriage.

Before we delve into the specifics, one key question does arise – does a change in the practice of marriage change the doctrine? This is a complex question, and one that deserves some attention. The potential doctrinal implications are usually brought up by those who are seeking, by any method possible, to prevent even discussion – let alone action – on opening marriage to two people of the same sex. The argument often goes along these lines: much of the Church of England's doctrine is found in its practices (following the adage *lex orandi, lex credenda* – what we pray, we believe), and if those practices change then this is ultimately a change in belief. This is a coherent argument, and must not be immediately dismissed, yet it is oversimplifying in the abstract what we know is not the case in practice – this would by no means be the only time that what occurs in practice is not that specifically described in the formularies of the Church, or indeed even in the Canons.

The Church of England has managed to hold a huge number of different – even contradictory – doctrinal positions within the same tent, because of the willingness of each different party to respect the integrity of the other and to live out a unity-in-diversity model that is well suited to a church that has (or at least aims to have) a presence in each community in England through the parish system. Of course, these parties have occasionally rubbed up against each other and even broken into open warfare, but nonetheless the centre of the Church has held. The Canons of the Church of England have not been made to face the impossible strain because there has been a widely held view that these Canons are not intended as a straitjacket for the Church and instead provide a guiding light for its polity and workings that can nonetheless adapt to circumstance. It is therefore somewhat curious that marriage has become the only issue where diversity cannot be tolerated.

We will return to the question of diversity in the final chapters, but for now it is worth recognising that there are a variety of answers to a variety of key questions across a variety of different churches, Church of England, Anglican and otherwise. At present, questions relate to the right ordering of the sacramental life, the ordination of women, the validity of ordination, the need for rebaptism – the list is endless. Yet it is also clear that whilst some of these things have led to an impaired communion, the general movement of ecumenism is one in which different churches gather around and eat together, even if not yet the holy meal of the Eucharist. Within the Church of England, it is certainly the case that even the happenings of the Eucharist cannot be agreed upon – the theology of different wings of the Church leading to fundamental differences in understanding as to what is going on at the holy table. Much is made of the devastating, splintering effect of any church accepting equal marriage, yet it appears that this is more talk than reality.

As more and more countries get to grips with the secular knowledge on this topic, the acceptance of the existence of – and eventually the celebration of – LGBTQI people is going to become more widespread rather than less. Certain factions within the Church most certainly want to erase the LGBTQI experience, but there is absolutely no evidence this will happen in the wider world. On a global level, LGBTQI people live happier and more fulfilled lives now than they have ever done, and there is no reason whatsoever to believe that the entire tide of the gradual and ever-increasing emancipation of the oppressed throughout history will turn. The Church can either choose to cover its eyes and ears and pretend this is not happening, or grapple with it – as this book urges the Church to do. But to dress up a refusal to engage in questions of 'doctrinal revisionism' or 'ecumenical concern' is to refuse to recognise the prophetic role that a church might be called to express. It may be that this is one of the gifts that the Church of England – like other churches before it – has to offer to the Church catholic, a gift that its modus of scripture, tradition and reason perfectly sets it up to do.

To return specifically to the doctrinal question – does this change the Church's doctrine? – the answer is both yes and no. Does it present a challenge to the Church's doctrine? Most certainly it does, and a challenge that is substantiated with action can most definitely be seen as a challenge that makes a claim on the truth (or otherwise) of the doctrine itself. Yet to allow a change in practice at this stage, without changing the words on the page of the Canons, is quite simply not to change the explicit doctrine of the Church irreversibly or fundamentally. Perhaps the best way to imagine what is happening is in the words used in the Church of Wales – it is experimental and optional, leaving the way forward open to the work of the Spirit and to a discernment of the fruits of any change. In essence, does such a change lead to more life in all its fullness, or less? Of course, arguments will rage around how this might be measured, but the thrust of this book's argument is that we must use all the gifts of God – scripture, tradition, reason, experience – to come to a mind on this. Experimental liturgies on the blessing of same sex marriages are a gift to the Church precisely because of this – and indeed, we already have access to the 'experiments' found in other churches which have blessed same-sex couples. In no case has there been any measurable loss to the lives of any of God's people – straight or LGBTQI – and in many cases, lives have flourished because of these blessings.

The problem with the word 'experimental' is that all kinds of fallacious arguments can be put forward that immediately call into question the 'Christian' nature of this experiment. The most classic of these, which is often presented in a variety of forms, states that this removal of 'boundaries' is a slippery slope. If we start to bless two men who express relational sexuality towards each other in a monogamous relationship, then the next thing we know, we'll be blessing threesomes or men marrying their dog. This does indeed sound ludicrous, but they are real arguments that were put forward during the debate on introducing civil equal marriage in the UK within the last ten years. The reality, of course, is that what is really at stake is where those boundaries are placed. These kinds of arguments are doubtless driven by fear – fear breeds panic, which itself breeds dishonesty, all in the name of preventing a greater evil from occurring, the blessing of same-sex couples. Yet what is really going on here is a fight about the policing of boundaries, with concern that those advocating same-sex blessings are re-making and re-marking those boundaries in a dangerous way. Ultimately, this is an argument about the fundamentals of what is being blessed, and thus what can be included within the boundaries.

It is from this that we hear the case laid out that we cannot simply redefine marriage, specifically in a way contrary to that found in scripture and tradition. The astute reader will already be several steps ahead and recognise the glaring omission in this argument. Yet to return to the arguments made in Section One of this book, it is important to lay out not only what the 'definition' has commonly been held to be, but also to think carefully about whether the blessing of same-sex couples really redefines anything, or whether it instead refines what is fundamental to the definition that we currently have for marriage.

Prior to any discussion of this, it is also key to enter any such discussion with an informed view of the history of marriage and the Church's relationship to this. It is beyond the scope of this book, but readers may find the writings of Professor Diarmaid MacCulloch instructive in this regard.[2] In short, that the Church has ever had one single view or practice of marriage – that of the twenty-first century wedding – is demonstrably untrue, and it is also abundantly clear that the relationship between the civil and the religious aspects of marriage have never been simple. Marriage practices across the world continue to exhibit significant differences, and the history of marriage within the Church of England does not suggest a simple definition. Nonetheless, we will consider the form of

---

[2] In addition, there is significant historical analysis in Thatcher, A., *The Oxford Handbook of Theology, Sexuality, and Gender*.

marriage in the Book of Common Prayer (the normative text and authorised liturgy of the Church of England) and in the more recent form of service *Common Worship* (an official alternative, and more widely used form of services) and identify the key threads of what is thought to occur and what marriage is thought to signify.

To turn first to the Book of Common Prayer's 'Solemnisation of Holy Matrimony'. The Preface is worth considering in full, as it gives an indication as to the meaning of 'solemnisation', and as to the underlying meaning of the marriage itself:[3]

> Dearly beloved, we are gathered together here in the sight of God, and in the face of this Congregation, to join together this man and this woman in holy Matrimony; which is an honourable estate, instituted of God in the time of man's innocency, signifying unto us the mystical union that is betwixt Christ and his Church; which holy estate Christ adorned and beautified with his presence, and first miracle that he wrought, in Cana of Galilee; and is commended of Saint Paul to be honourable among all men: and therefore is not by any to be enterprised, nor taken in hand, unadvisedly, lightly, or wantonly, to satisfy men's carnal lusts and appetites, like brute beasts that have no understanding; but reverently, discreetly, advisedly, soberly, and in the fear of God; duly considering the causes for which Matrimony was ordained.
>
> First, It was ordained for the procreation of children, to be brought up in the fear and nurture of the Lord, and to the praise of his holy Name.
>
> Secondly, It was ordained for a remedy against sin, and to avoid fornication; that such persons as have not the gift of continency might marry, and keep themselves undefiled members of Christ's body.
>
> Thirdly, It was ordained for the mutual society, help,

---

[3] *Book of Common Prayer (1662)* (Cambridge: Cambridge University Press, 2004).

and comfort, that the one ought to have of the other, both in prosperity and adversity. Into which holy estate these two persons present come now to be joined.

Before considering the similar elements from *Common Worship*, it is important to recognise that several elements of the Book of Common Prayer service appear problematic in the contemporary world, and it is for this reason that the service is infrequently used (and was thought to need updating in the form found in *Common Worship*). The first of these problems is found in the vows, in which the woman is asked to vow to obey and serve the man – a requirement that is not found in the man's vow. There is certainly biblical precedent for this – once again a full discussion can be found elsewhere – but it remains problematical given our developing human and biblical understanding.

The second key issue is surrounding procreation – something that is more sensitively discussed (and re-interpreted) in the *Common Worship* service we see below. Pro-creation moves from being solely about sexual intercourse leading to childbirth and takes on a wider meaning – a theme we will return to below. It is also interesting that marriage, according to the Book of Common Prayer, is closely associated with the couples' receiving of the Holy Communion, suggesting that marriage was not solely about the couple themselves but also about their incorporation and belonging to the community of faith. We shall touch on these themes in the next chapter, but it is interesting that there appears to be no similar essential liturgical connection made to the wider life of the Church in the modern Church of England for newly married couples. This may, of course, reflect the fact that couples can marry despite having no relationship or involvement with their local church community. This stands in stark contrast to the LGBTQI people who are active members of their church, and yet are forbidden this very rite.

The Common Worship marriage ceremony contains

similar but slightly different themes to those found in the Book of Common Prayer. The Preface states:[4]

> Marriage is a gift of God in creation
> through which husband and wife may know the grace
>   of God.
> It is given that as man and woman grow together in
>   love and trust,
> they shall be united with one another in heart, body
>   and mind,
> as Christ is united with his bride, the Church.
>
> The gift of marriage brings husband and wife together
> in the delight and tenderness of sexual union
> and joyful commitment to the end of their lives.
> It is given as the foundation of family life
> in which children are [born and] nurtured
> and in which each member of the family,
> in good times and in bad,
> may find strength, companionship and comfort,
> and grow to maturity in love.
>
> Marriage is a way of life made holy by God,
> and blessed by the presence of our Lord Jesus Christ
> with those celebrating a wedding at Cana in Galilee.
>
> Marriage is a sign of unity and loyalty which all should
>   uphold and honour.
> It enriches society and strengthens community.
> No one should enter into it lightly or selfishly
> but reverently and responsibly in the sight of almighty
>   God.

---

[4] *Common Worship* services are available here: https://www.churchofengland.org/prayer-and-worship/worship-texts-and-resources/common-worship/marriage.

N and *N* are now to enter this way of life.
They will each give their consent to the other
and make solemn vows,
and in token of this they will [each] give and receive a
    ring.

We pray with them that the Holy Spirit will guide and
strengthen them,
that they may fulfil God's purposes
for the whole of their earthly life together.

An alternative Preface is also offered by *Common Worship*:

We have come together in the presence of God, to witness the marriage of *N* and *N*, to ask his blessing on them, and to share in their joy. Our Lord Jesus Christ was himself a guest at a wedding in Cana of Galilee, and through his Spirit he is with us now.

The Bible teaches us that marriage is a gift of God in creation and a means of his grace, a holy mystery in which man and woman become one flesh. It is God's purpose that, as husband and wife give themselves to each other in love throughout their lives, they shall be united in that love as Christ is united with his Church.

Marriage is given, that husband and wife may comfort and help each other, living faithfully together in need and in plenty, in sorrow and in joy. It is given, that with delight and tenderness they may know each other in love, and, through the joy of their bodily union, may strengthen the union of their hearts and lives. It is given as the foundation of family life in which children may be born and nurtured in accordance with God's will, to his praise and glory.

In marriage husband and wife belong to one another, and they begin a new life together in the community. It is a way of life that all should honour; and it must not be undertaken carelessly, lightly, or selfishly, but reverently, responsibly, and after serious thought.

This is the way of life, created and hallowed by God, that N and N are now to begin. They will each give their consent to the other; they will join hands and exchange solemn vows, and in token of this they will [each] give and receive a ring.

Therefore, on this their wedding day we pray with them, that, strengthened and guided by God, they may fulfil his purpose for the whole of their earthly life together.

It is also worth considering the Pastoral Introduction to the Marriage Service which, whilst not formally part of the marriage ceremony itself, gives an indication as to what is believed by the Church of England about marriage:

Marriage is intended by God to be a creative relationship, as his blessing enables husband and wife to love and support each other in good times and in bad, and to share in the care and upbringing of children. For Christians, marriage is also an invitation to share life together in the spirit of Jesus Christ. It is based upon a solemn, public and life-long covenant between a man and a woman, declared and celebrated in the presence of God and before witnesses.

On this their wedding day the bride and bridegroom face each other, make their promises and receive God's blessing. You are witnesses of the marriage, and express your support by your presence and your prayers. Your support does not end today: the couple will value continued encouragement in the days and years ahead of them.

In the first instance, it is essential to recognise that the two key elements of a marriage ceremony held in a church are the blessing and the witnessing of the marriage. The Church of England also offers an authorised service for prayer and dedication after a civil marriage, but this service has no provision for the blessing of the couple of the marriage – it simply contains an optional blessing of the couples' rings that asks them to be 'a symbol of unending love and faithfulness and of the promises they have made to each other'. In addition, there are a number of optional elements in the service; if all are omitted, then the grounds given for marriage above are interestingly not included. The service itself is described as a consecration, and the couple pray 'that [God] may consecrate your marriage and empower you to keep the covenant and promise you have solemnly declared'. Such a service, then, is not a blessing, and would not fulfil what is being asked for when same-sex couples ask for the blessing of the Church.

It is key, then, to identify blessing as the fundamental point of disagreement between those in the Church who favour same sex unions and those who do not. The element of witness is certainly important, but for those who oppose equal marriage, the witness is somewhat irrelevant as they will claim that a marriage is not possible thus cannot be witnessed. The frequent refrain is that the Church cannot bless that which God does not call holy – which appears to be both the sexual and non-sexual relationships lived out by LGBTQI people. It is not consistent or clear why celibate friendships should not be blessed by the Church – not of course called marriage – but it is somewhat suggestive that beneath the theology lies more than a hint of homophobia. There is no good reason whatsoever to refuse to bless any friendship, yet despite frequent protestations that anti-LGBTQI churches are not homophobic, it is noticeable that no pastoral provision whatsoever has been drawn up to bless the celibate friendships that they so espouse.

Yet, to return specifically to relational sexuality, it is here that the dividing line has been most clearly drawn, and it is for this reason that those who oppose same-sex relational sexuality refuse to compromise. For them, belonging to a church that 'blesses sin' is a step too far, even if they refuse to 'bless the sin' themselves. A blessing can only be given to that which is good, and the corollary of their position is that these relationships do not embody good. Arguments around whether marriage is a sacrament are out of the scope of this book, but whether marriage is called a sacrament, sacramental or otherwise, at the heart of this union is something important and holy that is blessed by God, and which displays something of the being and love of God within itself. It is for this reason that it is blessed, and the out-workings of this blessing are described in some detail in the marriage services, to which we now turn.

It is these out-workings that are best able to point us towards an understanding of the nature of marriage. It is important to hold these up against the innately gendered language we associate with marriage to see whether such language is necessary. We learn that marriage is a gift of God, blessed by Christ – a gift freely given, we presume, to all (once again raising the question of how and why God would create people for whom this gift is dangled like a forbidden fruit) – and is a sign of the mystical union between Christ and His church. We are told that 'as man and woman grow together in love and trust, they shall be united with one another in heart, body and mind, as Christ is united with his bride, the Church.'[5] Arguments

---

[5] The imagery of 'heart, body and mind' and the becoming of 'one flesh' is a metaphor that points to both the love of God for the Church, and also the creation narratives found in the early chapters of Genesis (hence marriage is sometimes described as a 'creation ordinance') – a key example of this is found in the Book of Common Prayer which described marriage as (in part) 'an honourable estate, instituted of God in the time of man's innocency, signifying unto us the mystical union that is betwixt Christ and his Church'. Unless we are to take these chapters as literal historical fact (which is a vanishingly rare position to hold), then it is important that we do the work to interrogate and determine whether we are excluding marriage for same sex couples because it is genuinely incompatible with Genesis's theological narrative, or whether same sex relationships are simply not present as a contextual (rather than ontological) possibility in the minds of the writers. If we recognise that Genesis is an account that speaks of creation in a theological way, rather than a historical document, and that marriage *per se* is not mentioned in Genesis – but rather a form of relational sexuality is (as

have been put forward that force a link between the essential gendered nature of the couple and the imagery of Christ and His bride – frequently these arguments end in complementarian understandings of the married couple that emphasise the 'different but equal' roles of men and women. This not only ignores the basic science and rides roughshod over the complexity of human sexual difference we discussed in Chapters 4 and 5, but also takes representational, gendered difference - rather than the love of Christ for His church - as the starting point in the metaphor. The difference between Christ and His church can never be reduced to male-female binaries, and to do so cheapens and degrades a much more fundamental biblical truth.

Indeed, these arguments appear to do serious violence to the metaphor employed – it is both heterosexualist and patriarchal to assume that the man must take the role of Christ and the wife the role of the Church, yet this has far too often been used as an argument for the essentially gendered nature of marriage. A more sensitive and careful reading must surely alert us to the fact that neither partner in a marriage can ever truly represent Christ, but instead the metaphor works when we speak of the dynamic, growing, and deepening relationship between the couple as portraying and embodying in a bidirectional way the kind of love that unites Christ and his Church. It is here that they 'give themselves to each other in love throughout their

described in this chapter) – then we cannot easily disregard the possibility that this narrative might provide insights for same sex relational sexuality as well. Returning to the fact that marriage underwent a number of developments through Jewish and Christian history, and that the 'becoming one flesh' is most fully seen in the love of Christ for the Church, it would appear that there has not been a static understanding of the relationship between the Genesis 'creation ordinance' and human relationships, and that a determination to focus on the gender of the couple rather than the underlying theological truth it is trying to portray may itself be a dead end. An exploration of the context of Genesis – and its importance for interpretation – is found in Warner, M., 'Therefore a Man Leaves His Father and His Mother and Clings to His Wife': Marriage and Intermarriage in Genesis 2:24 *JBL* (2017) 136 (2): 269-288.

lives' so they are 'united in that love as Christ is united with his Church'. The gendered aspects come through reading this passage in the light of cultural preconceptions – the metaphor is weakened and impoverished, and the beauty of the marital relationship cheapened.

Indeed, one of the key elements of the relationship modelled – between Christ and His Church – is faithfulness. This faithfulness is not gendered, and nor does it solely relate to the sexual element of any relationship. It appears to cheapen the metaphor, therefore, to relate it to a gendered understanding where no such understanding is necessary. Faithfulness, one to the other, embraces the entire relationship and is one of the elements mentioned in the marriage service and most clearly seen in wider understandings of the marriage covenant. It is faithfulness between two people that is blessed and is a visible sign of God's working in and through a marriage, and it is simply untenable to suggest that faithfulness – and specifically that faithfulness exemplified in a marriage – can only be fully found in the relationship of two people of the opposite sex.

We then get to the key reasons given by the Book of Common Prayer – and developed through *Common Worship* – for the estate of Holy Matrimony. The first of these appears to be the most complicated to overcome – procreation. The Book of Common Prayer appears to restrict the definition of procreation to refer to sexual intercourse and childbirth, making reference to the bringing up of children as a separate event (nonetheless associated with marriage). *Common Worship* has softened this, as we have described, and describes marriage as the 'foundation of family life', and the parenthesis around the word 'born' is notable ('in which children are [born and] nurtured'), an attempt to recognise that not all marriage will (or will be able to) lead to childbirth, and thus making it clear that whilst childbirth is associated with marriage, it is not absolutely essential to its nature. It is not clear, on this reading, why same-sex couples are excluded, although an argument is made that it is the 'potential' rather than the actuality of childbirth that is required.

This is by no means obvious from the development of this text, and even a direct reference to the Book of Common Prayer does not suggest that procreation is an essential characteristic of marriage *per se* – the wording associates all childbirth with marriage, rather than the other way around, with marriage having been ordained as the rightful place for childbirth rather than childbirth being a prerequisite for genuine marriage. Yet to take a step back, it is abundantly clear that marriages that do not produce children nonetheless do provide a foundation for family life, and themselves can often be a 'creative relationship' that leads to mutual support and encouragement, and support and encouragement for friends and family alike (and this is to ignore the life-giving environment that same-sex marriages provide for the bringing up of children, which is clearly and unambiguously shown through the scientific and sociological literature). The Book of Common Prayer makes mutual society a category on its own, but it is clear that the direction of travel in *Common Worship* links these procreation with the formation and building up of mutual society in a way that enriches both concepts.

The 'creative' aspect of procreation also bears more consideration. Much is made of the importance of childbearing in the definition of procreation, yet it is not at all clear that such a term need be restrained in this way. Procreation suggests a participation in a creative act of God – in the case of sexual reproduction, pointing to the fact that the act of bearing children is a participation in the overarching creative work of God Himself. The intentional link that is made in *Common Worship*, and our wider understanding of the life-giving potential of relationships beyond simply producing more children, must make us reconsider what it is about the marriage that is so important for childbirth and childrearing in the first place. It appears, on reflection, that a marriage offers an environment of wider procreation – where life is enriched through participating in the work of God, in nurturing each other and wider society, and in the life-enhancing love that permeates a marriage. The gendered nature of marriage is irrelevant in this case, and yet this creative action appears to be at the very heart of the nature of marriage. Our human knowledge and experience show this to be the case; this is yet another example of the importance of the three-legged stool. Perhaps our slavish obsession with gendered language in marriage has hidden this insight, and this is a gift of the LGBTQI community to the refining and deepening of the theological enterprise.

The final characteristic of marriage that we encounter in the Book of Common Prayer is the avoidance of fornication – something rather less emphasised in *Common Worship*, which instead refers to the 'delight and tenderness of sexual union' and 'joyful commitment'. This need not detain us for long, as there is no good reason for this to be gendered whatsoever. Nonetheless, we know from the evidence and experience of LGBTQI people – Christians, even clergy (even bishops!), included – that sex between two people of the same sex can certainly lead to delight and tenderness, and there is no evidence beyond prejudice that suggests LGBTQI people are less able to embrace joyful commitment – in fact, it is the Church which appears currently to be opposing this!

This chapter is not written to be a comprehensive repudiation of traditionalist arguments, and nor is it designed to provide a full theology of same-sex marriage.[6] Indeed, one of the key points that it does make is that the theology of same-sex marriage may, in fact, simply refine and aid the understanding of opposite-sex marriages as well. Yet one key thing to note is that the fact something hasn't been done before is not a strong argument not to do it, however much we might appeal to tradition. We have seen, throughout this

[6] Readers may also be interested in Herbert, C., *Towards a Theology of Same-Sex Marriage* (London: Jessica Kingsley, 2020).

chapter, that rather than redefine, what the lives of LGBTQI people are doing is helping us refine our doctrines and our understanding of the human person. *Issues in Human Sexuality* turned Church of England discussions on sexuality into a conversation on repressive sexuality, and recent conversations about same-sex marriage have highlighted the weakness of current Church of England teaching and practice as relates to marriage. The lives of LGBTQI people is a gift to a church that desperately needs to develop a theology of relationship and relational sexuality.

It is, then, perhaps significant that it is in the alternative Preface to the marriage ceremony that we find a helpful and clear description of this relational sexuality – that makes clear the importance and complex relationship between the bodily, the emotional and the spiritual:

> It is given, that with delight and tenderness they may know each other in love, and, through the joy of their bodily union, may strengthen the union of their hearts and lives.

This is a very clear, and unambiguous, assertion of one of the key points raised on several occasions throughout this book – that it is a false dichotomy to separate the sexual from the rest of both the individual and relationship. It becomes increasingly challenging to argue that marriage – in which this ideal is situated – should be forbidden to individuals and their relationships simply by virtue of those individuals being attracted to someone of the same sex. Such individuals are not abnormal in their desires, longings, loves, ability to build up and live with delight and tenderness – the only unusual facet, compared to the norm, is their sexual preference for someone who happens to be the same sex that they are. There is simply no clear reason to withhold relational sexuality from them.

Yet despite all this, and in many ways because of a refusal to engage in the hard work of contextual theology that is required,[7] the Church has opposed and continues to oppose all sexual relationships between people of the same sex, whatever their contribution to mutual society, procreation, creativity, commitment, love and flourishing. The Church of England bishops were vehemently against civil partnerships when they were proposed, a history we shall consider in the penultimate chapter, and the same vitriol was turned on the introduction of equal marriage. Clergy may enter civil partnerships but not marry, and those in civil partnerships must agree to remain celibate. Yet the Church continues to expressly forbid the blessing of any kind of relationship between two people of the same sex – celibate or otherwise – despite allowing clergy to enter civil partnerships. The current situation is a mess, with the finger of blame pointing firmly at the structural and institutional homophobia of the Church, and unfortunately at its agents as well, the General Synod and the bishops. The Church of England's position – whatever its warm words – is shown in its actions, and in its disciplining of clergy of the same sex who marry, and its total refusal to bless any love between two people of the same sex, celibate or otherwise, it cannot claim to be anything else. It is a church of repression, erasure, abuse of power and exclusion, and yet this chapter has shown how it might turn the tide and develop a mature and life-giving theology of relationship. It remains abominable that the Church of England refuses to do the work required to enable it to properly minister to LGBTQI people in this way.

Indeed, ultimately the concept of marriage is a conservative one – and that arguments advanced

---

[7] Those who have actually engaged with the rich, varied and exciting literature in gender and sexuality studies (including queer theory), both within and without the theological realm, cannot help but be struck by the extreme position that is held when all this sociological, anthropological, psychological and biological interplay is neglected and rejected because of a narrow form of biblicism with which it cannot enter dialogue. This is not good theology, and it rejects the complex and dynamic nature of the scriptures themselves.

here are ones that seek to bring more people into the institution rather than bring about a genuine redefinition of sexual relationship. The arguments put forward here are arguments that favour expression, inclusion, openness, and a church that is a careful and just steward of power. At the very least, the Church of England should be open to blessing same-sex couples, if only to see what the fruits of the Spirit might be. In marriage it is the couple who are the ministers – the Church through its ministers simply witnesses and calls down God's blessing. It is time to allow the Holy Spirit to show us whether God will respond to that call for blessing or not. Ultimately, the blessing belongs to God, not the Church, and if He truly will not call same-sex couples blessed, then we will see it in their lives and in the life of the Church.

The truth is, of course, that marriage is already happening between people of the same sex, and has been for years – not civil marriage, although that is also happening, but rather the lived state of matrimony which the Church is called to witness and bless. In the past (and in some places, even today) such relationships were illegal, and yet the love of two people for each other remained and remains steadfast – a sacrament of the love of God for His church. It is not the role of the Church to 'own' marriage, but to witness – or recognise – it. This is all that is missing now; the current position of many churches is simply one of failed recognition, and failed witness to the work of the Holy Spirit. We see God's blessing in the lives of innumerable loving, committed LGBTQI people – a blessing that the Church continues to refuse to give. May God forgive the Church for denying that which is already in front of its eyes, and may God lead the Church into this truth – a truth that He has already entrusted to His beloved LGBTQI children.

11

THE TABLE OF WELCOME

In the last chapter, we saw something of the possibilities of grace that an openness to the Holy Spirit might gift the Church. A key dividing line between those who are open to the possibility that God might be blessing same-sex couples and those who are convinced that this is impossible is the willingness to take the courageous step of imagining LGBTQI people at the wedding feast in heaven as full guests, invited and beloved, rather than primarily defined by their 'wounded' sexuality. Of course, no Christian can claim to have anything other than some level of brokenness in their lives – in their relationships with each other and with God – yet some continue to believe that such brokenness can never be righted whilst LGBTQI people continue to express themselves sexually towards each other in a monogamous, loving relationship. Ultimately, these relationships either point towards heaven or they do not – they are either a prefiguring of the eternal banquet, or they are an insult towards it.

Given all we know about same-sex relationships and their fruits, it is extremely hard from a position of external critical analysis to deny that anything good comes from a same-sex marriage. They are places which demonstrate caring homes, loving relationships, and appear to have the same creative and beautiful potential as marriages of people of the opposite sex. The argument that the world will fall apart because of them has proven to be empirically incorrect; same-sex marriages, if anything, appear to be boringly similar to those between two people of the opposite sex. No marriage is perfect, and no marriage can ever truly be a representation of the love of Christ for His Church, yet nonetheless something of this love can be seen in the fruits and the love of a marriage. On these grounds alone, it is challenging to find any serious argument to differentiate between marriages based on the grounds of the sex of the participants. Fallacious arguments can be made about children – the obvious biological reality being that same-sex couples cannot engage in reproductive sexual intercourse with one another – yet there are plenty of opposite-sex marriages that do not bring forth children, and many same-sex marriages in which they are brought up with love, attention and joy.

This leaves those who oppose same-sex marriage (and same-sex relational sexuality) as appearing increasingly desperate in what seems to be a search for reasons to oppose these relationships. It is perhaps from this that the more angry and obnoxious claims about scripture emanate, where false claims are made about the clarity of the Bible, and the inevitability of certain textual interpretations. It is certainly the case that some self-identified conservative Christians do genuinely believe that the Bible is entirely opposed to same-sex relations in all their forms – others will argue from the point of view of Christian history and tradition. The issue is that this is not a valid Anglican method of discernment, and to continue to attempt to enforce this reading on the Church of England – and churches like it, which respect scripture, tradition and reason – is both disingenuous and ultimately nonsensical. The Anglican position calls us to hold up these three things against one another, and if we fail to do that, and indeed reject all that we experience and discover in our rational thought, then we are rejecting what sits at the very heart of Anglicanism.

What sits behind the refusal to engage with experience and reason is also not entirely clear, although there is doubtless some mixture of squeamishness about homosexuality and also fear. This fear is not an altogether bad thing – within this heady mix will be a fear of offending God, of going against His commandments, of going against two millennia of church practice and of being an arrogant generation that feels it knows all the answers. Yet whilst these are reasonable and, indeed, entirely appropriate fears to hold, nonetheless they are doubtless mixed up with other, far less honourable fears – fear of change, fear of taking positive risks, fear of the unknown. The problem is that these fears have so infrequently been pitted against the risks of *not* being open to the fact that the winds of change may in fact be the Holy Spirit at work. Some of these risks have been illustrated in these pages, but there is yet one more: we may be offending God in refusing to liberate the LGBTQI people in our midst. This may be the commandment that He is sending us today – or rather this may be how we best follow His command to love as He loves us – and we may be being arrogant in our refusal to do so, placing our solidified interpretations of scripture above the gift of the living Holy Spirit. It may be that God is calling us to refine what church practice looks like in the light of new developments, and yet we are slamming the door in His face. The corollary is not that God has changed His mind – far from it – but that God is leading us ever closer to His heart in His continual revelation in the world. It is not God who has been wrong – it is us – and yet we continue to refuse Him.

It would appear that the Anglican way gives us a head start in addressing these kinds of questions in a theologically serious manner. It is most certainly true that the Church cannot simply be battered around by the ever-changing winds of the secular world – everything must be weighed up, tried, and tested in the light of scripture and tradition – but this is no excuse for ignoring what God might be doing in the world, and for taking the 'signs of the times' seriously. Given all that we know – the overwhelming scientific and sociological consensus on LGBTQI human flourishing – it takes a certain amount of arrogance, refusal to see or troubling levels of certainty to refuse to at least be open to the idea that God might be doing something extraordinary in these relationships and for these people. In fact, what appears to be happening is a removal of the 'other' label that has been applied to LGBTQI people for many years – it seems that God is refusing to apply this and instead saying that LGBTQI people are children of God just the same as any others. This is a radical position to hold – it goes against hugely deep-seated prejudice, homophobia and structural violence done in the name of the Church – yet it may indeed be where God is leading us. It may be that God does indeed intend the same relational living and loving for each human being, irrespective of their genitalia.

If God is indeed saying this to us, then we must as a church pray deeply and hard about the way we have treated LGBTQI people and come to repentance. This is far more than an apology for homophobia – which is entirely warranted whatsoever God's plan is for sexual intercourse – but instead a genuine repentance or 'turning back' towards God. Writers from Girard to Volf have highlighted the danger of 'othering' in theological discourse and Christian self-understanding, and it appears to be part of the ever-present sin of pride and envy that clings so closely to the life of the Church.[1] As Christians, we appear to associate God with boundaries far more than God does Himself – we look for certainties, for binaries, for simple and simplistic ways of identifying who is 'in' and who is 'out'. This leads to a club mentality in Christianity which is deeply unattractive and causes significant challenge in our mission, yet it is a mentality that appears almost impossible to avoid. As Christians, we all-too-frequently try to create 'Christian' communities that look and behave just like us – mistaking our particular manifestations of the Christian life for the core of Christian living itself.

For a straight white man, for example, the way that a gay black woman can be viewed is various – she can be seen

---

[1] A starting point would be Girard, R., *The Scapegoat* (Washington DC: Johns Hopkins University Press, 1989) and Volf, M., *Exclusion and Embrace* (Nashville: Abingdon, 1996).

primarily as different, in race and sexuality, or she can be seen primarily and fundamentally as the same, as a child of God. This is not to attempt to obliterate our variety as humankind, or indeed to suggest that our differences do not affect our relationship to one another and the wider world (often due to deep seated prejudice), but it is to ask what difference Christianity makes to our relational self-understanding. Those who oppose same-sex sexual relationships may argue that they are not othering in their gaze, yet it is fundamentally othering to describe some people as unable to express themselves in relational sexuality by virtue of their innate and God-given self. We have seen that the fruits of this relational sexuality are empirically no different in nature between same-sex and opposite-sex couples – it is therefore a judgement call being made that such fruits are irrelevant to the question being asked, which appears a highly inconsistent conclusion.

Christians are called to reflect something of the love of God – indeed the love of the Trinity – in their lives, and in their relationships. To declare that one group of people cannot do this in the same way as others – contrary to all the evidence – is to 'other' them in a way that appears quite contrary to the creative will of God. An appeal to particular interpretations of biblical texts does not help us avoid facing this question head on – indeed, it is a question that gets to the heart of the character of the God that we worship and adore. If we cling to these interpretations, we appear to be faced with a God that appears to allow beauty and love – inseparable in nature from that found in opposite-sex marriages – to come from what we are told God calls grave sin and will not bless, or a God whose revelation is fundamentally inconsistent. We are also faced with a God who created some humans to be unable to reflect His love in ways that others can – in essence, we have a God who has created the 'other'. This is not the God of the Bible or Christian tradition.

There is, of course, an argument that God does indeed allow some people to be born who cannot reflect this love and relationship. Amongst them might be those who desire sexual relationship but do not find it, although this is a false argument as their situation is fundamentally different to LGBTQI people – LGBTQI people are told they cannot reflect the love and relationship because of who they are by nature, in a way that is forever unchanging. In fact, those who seek but do not find love are more of an argument for the proposition – such love is clearly something that many seek as part of their human experience, a human experience that reflects something of the Godhead. Those who do not find such love are not in some way less of a walking sacrament – this is not the inevitable corollary of a high view of relational love. We are not talking here of the actual expression of sexual love, but rather its potential – a potential that may remain unfulfilled in many people of different sexualities, and which may prove painful or difficult. It is the denial of this potential in LGBTQI people that is fundamentally different, and it is this denial that appears so blasphemously 'othering'.

An alternative group might be those called to be celibate, but this argument too is fallacious – such a calling is itself a gift of God to reflect something of the love and relationship of God in a different way. Yet such a calling is not something involuntarily imposed on a group of people – it is something discerned, grappled with and ultimately recognised as a gift of God to an individual. A final group are those with genuinely disordered sexual proclivities, the disorder lying in an inability to form sexual connection in a way that would reflect God's inner love and relationship – an example being paedophilia. The existence of this disorder is a tragedy – it leads to untold suffering and pain, both for those who are victims of this grave sin and indeed often for the perpetrators themselves. Yet the acting on this impulse is a sin because it does not reflect the love and grace of God, and it is a disorder – an illness – because it is the orientation of a bodily function in a way that harms, both the individual (most particularly psychologically) and the victim.

That God allows disease and suffering is a valid question – albeit beyond the scope of this book – but it is a fundamentally different question to that we are addressing. There is no reason whatsoever to refer to homosexuality as an illness – all serious scientific and sociological work on this topic agrees. Yet what is fascinating is that in the 'othering' of LGBTQI people, this is what the Church appears to do. Same-sex sexual expression is categorised as an illness in Christian terms because, according to the received wisdom, God does not permit it under any circumstances – relational or otherwise – and it is therefore a major aberration from the right functioning of the body. This is a very strong claim indeed – especially given the evidence, none of which points in this direction. Whilst the Church of England does not talk in these terms, this is nonetheless the inevitable conclusion that must be drawn. It is not hard to see how the words of the Primate of Nigeria – referring to homosexuality as a 'virus' – have come about, given this kind of analysis.

The key place in the Christian life where othering is so clearly seen to be blasphemy is at the Eucharist. Whilst some denominations continue to make gathering at the table contingent on club membership of their particular Christian club, one of the great gifts of Anglicanism to the wider church catholic is the openness of the Eucharistic feast to all the baptised. This baptism – freely given – is something open to LGBTQI people and others alike – and takes the whole person and claims them for Christ. At the Eucharistic gathering, all are equal before God, welcome as guests of Christ at his table. Guests flourish precisely because of this welcome – Christians meet, listen, talk, and learn without placing themselves in the high places or claiming the place of host. At the Eucharist, they eat together, learning more about the love of Christ in word and sacrament; they repent of their waywardness and sin; they make peace with one another; they proclaim the faith; they hear and contemplate scripture; they pray for one another and the world; they are sent out into the world as living and loving witnesses to the saving power of Christ. Their definition is given by Christ, not by any church party or interpretation. Christ is the head of the household.

LGBTQI Christians who come to the table are welcomed in the same way as any other – or at least, they should be. Yet if we take the Eucharist as our starting point and as the exemplar of Christian living, how many LGBTQI people could truly describe their experience of the Church as Eucharistic? LGBTQI people, as we have seen, are talked at and about, rather than with; scripture is employed against them at the expense of their experience – the word placed inappropriately and implacably against the sacrament; they are not listened to but lectured to; and all too frequently the place of the host is usurped by those who claim to know the mind of Christ above the rest of the community that is gathered. They are told not to behave the same way as other people – in a responsible and God-oriented expression of relational love – but instead told to do the very opposite of what they feel called to do by God. They are then 'othered', posited as the problem and the scapegoat, and chased away from the table in the name of unity. They are called equal, and yet the structural and societal imbalances that work against them are not named or accounted for. And yet they keep coming to the table because God keeps calling them to His feast.

There are two things to consider, when reviewing this appalling record of the allegedly Eucharistic community and its relationship to its own LGBTQI members. The first is that this experience of LGBTQI people could actually prove extremely valuable to the Church corporate, if only it would listen rather than point fingers, decry division and ask LGBTQI people to speak with 'cool heads and warm hearts'. The experience of the marginalised so often speaks to the behaviour of the centre, and in this case it casts a light on what being a truly Eucharistic church might look like in practice. The Eucharist is not simply something for a Sunday morning – it is the lifeblood of the Church, and a model of living that must permeate and define the Christian life. LGBTQI people not only suffer the consequences of a failure in this way of life: they point towards the truths that lie at the heart of it, refining and clarifying them. As we saw previously, the Church has far too often focused on the peripheral when considering the things that define it – in its definition of marriage, its reading of scripture, and in its development of a Christian anthropology. LGBTQI people – like so many other oppressed groups who still cling to the cross of Christ – are part of the solution, if only the Church would recognise them as full members of the body of Christ, rather than as diseased and sinful offshoots.

The second consideration is an entirely obvious one: the Eucharist – and Eucharistic living – already gives us the model for engagement within the Church – and we might argue, gives an indication as to the right ordering of engagement without as well. Thinking back to the principles of the second Section of this book, it is clear that Eucharistic living promotes the things that are good and rejects those that cause damage – Eucharistic living is a life and attitude of openness, expression, vulnerability and good stewardship of power, and ultimately inclusion under the banner of Christ. It is a way of life that, when lived intentionally, can fundamentally change the tone of the debate and difficulty in the contemporary church, and it is a form of life that the experience of LGBTQI people points us towards. Repentance, peace and reconciliation, scriptural contemplation, proclamation, sending out, recognising the Lord in the breaking of the bread and in the life of his people – all this is Eucharistic living, and all this fosters that life of inclusion under Christ. That way may not be simple, and will often provide more contingencies than certainties, but this is the way of Christ.

As God told Job, He does not have to answer our questions on our terms – we are foolish to seek absolute clarity where there is none. Yet He remains God, and in the life and death of His Son He gave us hope – a hope infused with faith and love. This hope is at the heart of the Eucharistic vision, and in giving the Eucharist to His church, Jesus called us to love as he loves us – neighbours and enemies alike. A call to love one's enemies is no easy ask – and is not the same as demanding we give into abuse and violence, or self-flagellate in a vague and dangerous attempt to become friends, unconditionally, with those who despise us. Far too often, LGBTQI people – and other despised and rejected groups – are told to shoulder abuse on top of their oppression, and to model a self-denying love towards others which is ultimately a cover for more abuse. At worst, this is simply a tool of the oppressor, who claims 'hurt' from the pain that emanates from the very wounds that they have inflicted on their victims – a false hurt that is nothing more than the surprise when their verbal lacerations cause a victim to howl in agony. At best, it is the misguided and utterly uninformed opining of the unaffected onlooker, who calls for 'calm on both sides' and fails to recognise the huge power and structural imbalances at play. Unless and until the Church – and other oppressive organisations – recognise the lack of equivalence between the hurt felt in the oppressor and oppressed, and recognise the continued violence that such an attitude actively sponsors, then there is no hope for genuine listening, let alone reconciliation. The aura of malicious woundedness that 'conservatives' have employed for many years in their attacks on the dignity of LGBTQI people must be called out – a failure to do so is nothing less than complicity in the violence that they inflict.

True love in the Church is a whole reorientation and resituating of our lives, that demands our entire being, and yet which ultimately builds up the lover and the beloved. For the Church to embody this love requires the Church to be a place of honesty and integrity, in which truths are named and structural violence destroyed. Fundamentally, it is a place where the oppressed are raised up and not a place where the oppressed are asked – once again – to bow down to the oppressor. It is a place of reconciliation, yet a reconciliation that ultimately requires humility and honesty before the throne of grace. The Eucharist belongs to Christ, and it is to his rule that we submit, and not the loudest or most powerful voices in the Church. Eucharistic living demands reverence for Christ, and this reverence means being sensitive to and working to right the wrongs that remain in power imbalances and injustice at the heart of the Church. The Five Marks of

Mission need each other – and the fourth, 'to transform unjust structures of society, to challenge violence of every kind and pursue peace and reconciliation' must start within the Church itself.[2] Without this, the Church cannot be anything more than a resounding gong or clanging cymbal.

Embodied in such humility and honesty must be a commitment to name and strike down the straw men, false dichotomies, incoherent demands, and outright lies that continue to be told about the lives, requests and loves of LGBTQI people. Any Church is to some degree political, but this is not an excuse for behaving in a dishonest way that favours obfuscation rather than openness. Emotional manipulation, theologies of disgust, false dichotomies about the role of Spirit and scripture, voices of division that demand 'my way or the high way', arrogant false certainties about singular valid scriptural interpretations, bombastic and violent talk, unfounded claims of rife, rampant and inevitable promiscuity, demeaning and deliberately offensive language, misrepresentation, outright lies – all of these find no place in the life of a Eucharistic community, yet all have been seen in recent democratic processes in the Church.

Of course, there will remain disagreements, some of which will continue to cause great hurt and difficulty, but these disagreements must be discussed and honoured in good faith, with genuine attention paid to the imbalances of power that will inevitably exist. The Church must finally take some responsibility for the damage that it has done, and work to model a future that not only tends to the wounds but heals them too. This can never be a church of the powerful and of the oppressor – it must be a church where the radical equality that is preached is truly lived, an equality that does not simply come about by calling people equal. Radical equality means serious attention paid to the dynamics of community and individuals, and steps taken to mitigate the imbalances. The time for action is well overdue.

[2] https://www.anglicancommunion.org/mission/marks-of-mission.aspx.

A Eucharistic life is one in which the evangelical virtues of faith, hope and love are clearly seen – in the life of individuals, in their relationships, and in the whole make-up of the Church, internal and external. These three virtues have been sorely lacking in so much of the debate on LGBTQI inclusion. Instead, fear, a demand for certainty, and a deficit of love have been much more visible in the attitudes shown towards LGBTQI people. It is these three virtues, however, that best declare confidence in Christ and in the Holy Spirit's work in the Church and the world. If we looked for the Spirit's work with more hope, faith and love, and less fear, certainty and hatred, then we would most surely find the Spirit at action more readily and more often.

Ultimately, we are a church guided by the Holy Spirit and beloved by Christ. We may indeed make mistakes, and we will certainly continue to have disputes among us – but these must be reckoned with in the light of our Eucharistic existence. Whilst some might speak of the need for a universal church council to resolve our difficulties, surely it is the place of each church, wherever it is found, to try to ever resemble that Eucharistic perfection more and more. It is at the Eucharist that the Gospel is proclaimed in the centre of the assembly of God, and it is in Eucharistic living that we might best listen to what the Spirit is telling us through word and sacrament.

12

INTIMATE TRUTH

Over the past two chapters, we have begun to glimpse a different way of living our lives as Christians. In our discussions on marriage, we have seen a worked example of the importance of openness to the work of the Holy Spirit in our churches, and a willingness to dialogue with human knowledge and experience in our contemplation on both scripture and tradition. As we think about being a Eucharistic community, we dare to embrace hope – hope that is embedded in a community of faith and love, a community that comes to the table of God as His guests. Guests are welcomed by the host and treated with a radical equality that we can only ever hope to match. Yet this hope is at the heart of that community – and hope is at the centre of this book as well. Hope and reconciliation come through humility, honesty, and truth-telling.

For some, the bleak picture painted in the second section of this book will be seen as little more than an attack on the Church. Nothing could be further from the truth. The purpose of lifting the lid on the unhealthy culture and individual turmoil is to start to shine light where there is none, and to make a clarion call for change. At present, far too many individuals – many of them senior – are either too scared or simply unwilling to open this box. The reasons for this are multiple, and often overlapping – indeed, for some, the reasons will be a mixture of conscious and unconscious. Some argue that love and loyalty to the Church is more important than these 'difficulties'; some genuinely believe that there are no cultural problems whatsoever; others talk endlessly in terms of politics without ever outlining how this leads to the furthering of the kingdom; still others are so used to the current situation that they sit within it like victims of Stockholm Syndrome.[1]

We will consider the implications of the argument that 'there are more important things to worry about' in more detail below, but for now we must ask ourselves the question – are there really more important things than the health of the organisation that claims to be the body of Christ? These pages have shown not only that LGBTQI lives are being blighted, but that the whole life of the Church is disfigured by our culture and our behaviour towards one another. The lives of LGBTQI people are simply a lens through which the Church can be viewed, and what we have seen has not always been pretty. Yet to try to brush this all under the carpet, or claim that the situation is overblown, is not to love the Church – it is to destroy her. We do not build up the Church through half-truths, wink-wink nudge-nudge denials and through turning a blind eye to the evil within.

This is, ultimately, sin – leaders in the Church who refuse to listen are, by commission and omission, doing violence to the very body that they claim to love, and over which they have oversight. This is the very opposite of what the writer of the letter to the Ephesians (4:11-13) tells us the gifts of Christ were for:

> The gifts he gave were that some would be apostles, some prophets, some evangelists, some pastors and teachers, to equip the saints for the work of ministry, for building up the body of Christ, until all of us come to the unity of the faith and of the knowledge of the Son of God, to maturity, to the measure of the full stature of Christ.

---

[1] The well-known, albeit not clearly classified, state of being in which hostages develop a psychological attachment or bond with those who have taken them captive.

We have reached a crisis point in the Church – not a crisis driven by the divisions over 'orthodox' and 'unorthodox' teaching on sexuality, but a crisis at the heart of how we live as a church and how we engage with one another and the wider world. Yet this crisis is not inevitable, and nor is it final – indeed, it cannot be, if the Church truly is the body of Christ. We must face this crisis head on and stop obfuscating or denying its reality. At the centre of the declarations made in the order for the Ordination and Consecration of a Bishop in *Common Worship*, we find these lines:[2]

> Will you promote peace and reconciliation in the Church and in the world; and will you strive for the visible unity of Christ's Church?
> Will you be gentle and merciful for Christ's sake to those who are in need, and speak for those who have no other to speak for them?

For far too long, one part of these lines – 'the visible unity of Christ's Church' – has been prioritised above all of the rest. We still hear bishops and other senior clergy talk about the need for 'unity' above all else, and 'unity' – whether within the Church of England or the wider Anglican Communion – has been employed as the reason for continuing the oppression of LGBTQI people within the Church. The problem is that however much 'visible unity' we may claim to have, the reality is that this is nothing more than a mirage. The Church of England – and many other churches – do not have unity on the issue of relational sexuality for LGBTQI people, and what we currently describe as unity is in fact structural oppression. The tragic fact is that many of our bishops and clergy are themselves victims of this oppression, and yet remain paralysed and unable – and in some cases unwilling – to bring about the liberation that is needed.

---

[2] https://www.churchofengland.org/prayer-and-worship/worship-texts-and-resources/common-worship/ministry/common-worship-ordination-0.

The key to that liberation is found in the other parts of these two declarations – a commitment to the promotion of peace and reconciliation, a commitment to the gentleness and mercy shown to those who are in need, and a commitment to be the voice for the voiceless. The shocking unwillingness of those in authority to be this voice – a voice in the wilderness, perhaps, but a voice nonetheless – is scandalous, and is made more so when the reason given for this silence is the cause of unity. With a few honourable exceptions, this silence is deafening – from leaders who are LGBTQI and those who are not. Yet this is the very thing that Jesus Christ commands us to do:

> This is my commandment, that you love one another as I have loved you. No one has greater love than this, to lay down one's life for one's friends.
>
> (John 15:12-13)

This is at the very crux of our faith, and a church that lacks this kind of lifeblood is very sick indeed. Much is made of sacrificial leadership, but the sacrifice that we ask of our senior clergy – to remain silent, to live lives mired in untruths and half-truths, to be unable to speak out of fear of disunity – is not the sacrifice that God is asking of his church. If we are to ever move forward, we must set our bishops free – we must adopt an episcopal liberation theology, in which the entire people of God commend our bishops when they speak for all those who have no other to speak for them, and who strive for genuine unity through peace and reconciliation. Bishops should be able to talk about these issues in a way that respects their theological integrity and in which they are able to be genuinely honest, without threats of retribution. Indeed, the output of our bishops on this topic should be much more than corporate statements that simply repeat the party line. Relationships are central to lives lived in the Kingdom of God, yet bishops appear unable to speak personally and honestly about their own thinking on this. The only comments made are joint reiterations of 'church teaching' with no discussion welcomed, and LGBTQI once again have no one to listen to them, let alone advocates.

It is no longer good enough for LGBTQI people to be left off the list of the voiceless for whom church leaders speak. We have previously referred to the lack of moral voice that the Church has in the wider world given its position on LGBTQI people. In recent years, the voice of church leaders has become much louder on social issues – amongst them the plight of the poor, refugees and asylum seekers, the rights and basic human dignity of people of colour – yet, whilst the Church has frequently been found wanting in its own relationship with these groups, it has been extraordinarily unwilling, in the main, to include LGBTQI people within its groups of the oppressed to be raised up. This is unacceptable, whatever the underlying theology – even for those who oppose same-sex relationships, LGBTQI people have innate human dignity, and to fail to go into bat for them is inexplicable. Doing so would, of course, make even clearer how the Church's current positioning and theological approach (indeed, temerity) in fact contribute to the oppression of LGBTQI people themselves, yet this is something which can only benefit from the light of day.

To address the challenges of the current church fully and genuinely – a church which is riven with disunity – thus requires all of us involved in its life to face the reality of the situation head on. We have heard much of 'good disagreement' in recent years, but at the heart of being able to disagree effectively and appropriately is attention to, naming of and action to combat the underlying structural imbalances that have been illustrated throughout this book. This certainly applies to bishops, but it also applies to anyone who is engaged in these debates, and indeed anyone who wishes to play a part in the life of the Church. We will be unable to grapple with understanding and respecting LGBTQI people and their identity if we do not address the fundamental power imbalances, and indeed abuses of power, that our structures and our debates continue to embody. We will be unable to meet LGBTQI people on equal terms if we do not do the work to make those terms equal – and this means taking genuine and intentional action to tackle the imbalances within our culture and zealously combat our culture of fear, repression, and exclusion.

Heart cannot speak unto heart when the hearts of LGBTQI are held in chains. Equality requires action rather than warm words, and this action is going to be uncomfortable for some of those who have become comfortable with the *status quo*. This will include some LGBTQI people, who have been lulled into a false sense of powerlessness which suits those who wish to oppress them and keep them in fear. Primarily, however, it is going to be uncomfortable for those who benefit from the current power imbalances – however unconsciously – and for whom such change is a genuine threat to their hegemony and control.

It is very easy to lecture others on their sexuality when this teaching does not affect you directly – thus it is somewhat understandable that straight people cannot quite understand what it is that they are asking LGBTQI people to do or, rather, forbidding them to do. It is not that 'conservative' teaching has nothing to say to straight people and their sexuality – far from it – but the key difference is the total prohibition on any form of sexual expression whatsoever that is demanded from LGBTQI people (as murky a concept as this is, as we have discussed previously). The sheer cruelty of this position cannot be overstated, and nor can the cruelty of the blitheness with which it is so often proclaimed, despite the hand-wringing. This is ultimately a life-depriving demand – one that makes human experience lesser, rather than greater – and this makes it even more atrocious that this demand has become the test of orthodoxy for certain factions in the Church. To use other people's lives – lives that you cannot even begin to imagine – as this test is shameful and remains so unless it is incontrovertible that you are correct.

The frequent reference to the 'woundedness' of

'conservatives' when this position is challenged (as we described in the previous chapter) is extremely trying, and the false equivalence between disagreement on a theological position and the questioning of the entire identity of LGBTQI people needs to be consistently called out. The continued pushing, and frequent acceptance, of this false equivalence is simply another example of the structural oppression that lies at the heart of the Church. LGBTQI people and those who argue against their relational sexuality are not facing equivalent volleys and are not invested in these conversations in the same way – the debate for one is the entire life of the other, a life which is plucked out and made the topic of a debate by the Church in which all are declared welcome and equal. This is not ultimately a political issue – it is a personal one, and thus a deeply theological one. To fail to see the difference in stakes here is to be wilfully ignorant – to fail to try to address them is both cruel and negligent.

It is for this reason that open discussions and debates about the current position of the Church are key, although far too often the onus for this lies on the shoulders of LGBTQI people themselves. Much has been written in the wider literature about the important of allies – people who come alongside and help share the burden of the oppressed, who speak up for them and help take some of the flak when they are attacked. Allies are essential in this debate – not people who claim to somehow speak for LGBTQI people, but people who stand and speak alongside them. To be a true ally to the oppressed is a worthy calling – it requires humility, courage, openness and a willingness to listen to the experience of those you walk alongside. It is a ministry of allyship to which our straight bishops, clergy and laity are called, yet it is far too often a ministry that is too hard for them to bear.

The current position of the Church of England as relates to Civil Partnerships creates a significant tension in this regard – and once again a tension that falls on the shoulders of LGBTQI people. At present, clergy are permitted to enter into same-sex civil partnerships but on the understanding that these remain celibate (an understanding that requires the individual to give assurance to their bishop);[3] likewise, they cannot have these partnerships blessed, according to the specific and explicit 'pastoral statement' released by the House of Bishops. Whilst the bishops talk about pastoral and sensitive responses to civil partnerships, this is little more than a smokescreen – these partnerships may not be blessed, and because of this the bishops are refusing to call them good. As the Primates statement of 2003 stated (echoed in the bishops of the Church of England's response to Civil Partnerships):[4]

'The question of public rites for the blessing of same sex unions is still a cause of potentially divisive controversy. The Archbishop of Canterbury spoke for us all when he said that it is through liturgy that we express what we believe, and that there is no theological consensus about same sex unions. Therefore, we as a body cannot support the authorisation of such rites'.

[3] The situation became more tricky in 2019, when Civil Partnerships were opened to opposite sex couples. The Church of England published guidance on this (https://www.churchofengland.org/news-and-media/news-and-statements/civil-partnerships-opposite-sex-couples) stated that the 'ambiguity about the place of sexual activity' means that it was not possible 'for the church to unconditionally…accept civil partnerships as unequivocally reflecting the teaching of the church', and hence 'clergy of the Church of England should not provide services of blessing'. The statement drew clergy's attention to 'the teaching of the church on sexual morality, celibacy, and [their emphasis] the positive value of committed friendships', and made it clear that the entering of a Civil Partnership made it fair game for the church to ask awkward questions (paragraphs 23-25). The document also shows the mess that occurs when sophistry is applied to the nature of the different forms of relationship (particularly paragraphs 26-28), and is it not clear that the bishops themselves fully understood the difference in relationship that they attempted – unsuccessfully – to outline. A final element of interest from this statement is in paragraph 7, which states 'it has always been the position of the Church of England that marriage is a creation ordinance, a gift of God in creation and a means of his grace'. Unwittingly, the bishops have shown why the Anglican position is so cruel – do we truly believe LGBTQI people are by their nature excluded from this access to the grace of God?
[4] https://www.anglicannews.org/news/2005/07/house-of-bishops-issues-pastoral-statement-on-civil-partnerships.aspx.

This is not to say that practice necessarily follows theory. At present, civil partnerships are certainly being blessed, although on each occasion the blessing is either a fudge (with the appearance of being something else) or a courageous act by a single priest who risks censure and possibly their entire ministry. For some clergy, civil partnerships have replaced the dream of a marriage, and as we saw in our chapter on marriage, the relationships that they often embody are marriages already – they have just not been recognised by the Church as such. Yet this situation that we currently live within points to the tension – that those who favour blessing the lives and loves of LGBTQI people must navigate how to both name what the Church is doing, whilst at the same time live lives of joyful resistance.

The complexity of the situation is described by this clergyperson who is in a Civil Partnership:

'My problem mostly arises when people on the periphery of the Church – perhaps those coming in to use the church hall, or who I meet in some of the civic parts of my job, talk to me about my other half. I face this huge dilemma – do I refer to this as a marriage or am I honest and call it a Civil Partnership? I mean, what does honesty even mean in that situation – we are married, in all but name. So, in a sense, I want to just say 'yes we are married', because – for all intents and purposes, we are.

But there's this niggling part of me that says 'but you're not married'. And that's not some kind of self-doubt or internalised homophobia. It's more that I want to stand up and say 'this is what the Church has done to me, and it's not OK'. I feel like every time I say I am married, then it normalises what is a totally abnormal situation. We weren't allowed to have any ceremony in church, we weren't really allowed even to have our rings blessed, although one of my priest friends did it nonetheless.

So every time people ask me 'are you married?', I

feel both of these emotions at the same time – they're both valid. Yes, I am married, and my life is that of a married person, and I want to normalise that and live as a married couple; but brutally, no, I'm not married, because the Church refuses to allow me to be. Or it refuses to call what I am married and would sack me if I did. If we stay silent about that, it'll never change. There's something really cruel about being put in this situation, and I don't think straight clergy really get it.'

Another clergyperson speaks of the double-life they are asked to pursue:

'The thing is, of course we are expected to be celibate, but that's a requirement on me, not on my partner, and it just doesn't seem fair to him to make him do that. I mean, it's a bit of an open secret that a lot of us in civil partnerships are not celibate – and it's also true that a lot of clergy do try to keep that celibacy, out of obedience to the Church, and it breaks them. I'm not going to judge either group, because it's the situation the Church puts us in which is so pernicious, not the clergy.

Yet if I go to diocesan events, we end up with the usual talking around the topic, and God help me when the delicate discussions around twin or double bedrooms kick off. At the same time, the bishop invites me and my husband to dinner with him and offers us the spare double room. It's all faintly ridiculous, but it's hardly Christlike. We seem to suffer from a total inability to be honest with one another – I don't just mean my husband and me, but the bishops too! How can they have one line in public and another in private? It's shameful.'

It is worth noting that were the identity of this last clergyperson revealed, then they could face losing their ministry – despite the clear integrity which shines through their words. The problem is that the current situation encourages clergy and laity alike into open collusion with a system that is fundamentally broken and fundamentally dishonest. It ultimately encourages hypocrisy and punishes integrity, and it forces clergy, in particular, to treat their personal lives as political. Civil partnerships are clearly both marriages and not marriages, depending on the slant – and it is dehumanising to force clergy in them to continually navigate this political line whilst ultimately wanting to celebrate the love they have with their husband or wife.

The history of the Church's response to civil partnerships and equal marriage is indeed a shameful one – one filled with inconsistencies and political machinations that ultimately reflect extremely poorly on the institution. Lest we forget, whilst the Church of England has been more positive about civil partnerships in recent years, their original position was to vociferously oppose them – a position they then transferred to equal marriage, which was an entirely civil, rather than religious, affair. The bishops of the Church of England conveniently forgot their opposition to civil partnerships, it appears in order to be even more strident in their opposition to the 'redefinition' of marriage. Indeed, for some time there was a moratorium in place on clergy in civil partnerships being permitted to be elected bishop, although to date it appears that the lifting of this moratorium is primarily in theory rather than the practice (at least in terms of any kind of public announcements of civil partnership). Yet when this was lifted, the language used by the then chairman of Reform (and now a bishop in the Church of England), Rod Thomas, is revealing:[5]

> 'It will be much more divisive than what we have seen over women bishops. If you thought that was a furor, wait to see what will happen the first time a bishop in a civil partnership is appointed.'

[5] https://www.reuters.com/article/us-religion-gay-idUSBRE9030TS20130104.

It is hard to see how this is anything but a very poorly veiled threat.

Of course, it is easy to get lost within the rhetoric, and to end up inadvertently giving the impression that civil partnerships are less than they are for clergy who enter them. For many clergy who do enter a civil partnership, they do so with the same aims, joy, and devotion that straight clergy enter marriages. It is quite clear that for clergy in civil partnerships, the description of them as mere 'friendships' is little short of offensive, and we must be careful not to cast aspersions on those who have made their promises to each other and are committed, loving, monogamous couples living their lives together under God. Debates around equal marriage can occasionally veer into this kind of language, and it is key to avoid heaping any more judgemental opinions on those who have chosen to live their lives together in this way.

That all said, we must return to the fact that the Church of England still forbids the blessing of any same-sex relationship, and forbids any formal ceremony from taking place within a church building. The formulation of a civil partnership is fundamentally different to a marriage, in the required legalities and ceremonials, and whilst some people may include vows in their ceremonies, these are not required. It is for this reason that the Church of England can continue to pretend that they are nothing more than the formalisation of friendships.

For those clergy who choose to enter a civil marriage – rather than civil partnership – the rules are, however, fundamentally different. Blessings remain expressly forbidden, and the position of the Church of England is clear when it comes to clergy:[6]

---

[6]   From the House of Bishops Pastoral Guidance on Same Sex Marriage as issued 15/02/2014 (readers may be either amused or bemused that this statement first reached dioceses on Valentine's Day 2014) https://www.churchofengland.org/news-and-media/news-and-statements/house-bishops-pastoral-guidance-same-sex-marriage.

The House [of Bishops] is not, therefore, willing for those who are in a same sex marriage to be ordained to any of the three orders of ministry. In addition it considers that it would not be appropriate conduct for someone in holy orders to enter into a same sex marriage, given the need for clergy to model the Church's teaching in their lives.

This statement leaves no room for doubt whatsoever, and its practical out-working means that those who do enter marriages with someone of the same sex whilst an ordinand will not be ordained, and as a clergyperson, will not be granted any further license by the Church of England. Equal marriage is without question the end of ministry for LGBTQI clergy in the Church of England.

This brings into question the somewhat thorny topic of open disobedience to the discipline imposed by bishops. As we have already discussed, there are already places where such disobedience is being practiced – it is simply not compatible with the current position to offer a blessing for a civil partnership, yet these are occurring. They may be occurring entirely openly – in a stance of defiance – or they may be occurring covertly, making the most of the embarrassment and lack of willing for bishops to intervene in some dioceses. This is simply reflective of the overall culture of dishonesty and half-truths in which we currently live, in which a geographical patchwork of 'supportive' bishops and those who are more set on enforcing the rules create a post-code lottery. The same is true when it comes to demands for 'assurance' that civil partnerships are celibate. The overarching result of this kind of culture is one in which integrity is sacrificed on the altar of convenience.

That is not to say that blessing same-sex partnerships in this covert way is necessarily a bad thing – but this is not ultimately a sustainable position, despite the changes in culture that it might bring about by stealth. It is a tragedy that clergy are forced into this kind of behaviour, and it is also clear that the finger of blame lies with those who impose arbitrary and unjust rules. The reality is that individual bishops – or the leadership as a whole – could stop sacking and disciplining clergy straight away, without requiring an Act of Synod, but this requires a courage that does not appear to currently exist. Whilst there are arguments around whether it is right to offer a blessing on behalf of the Church when the Church refuses the blessing as a corporate body, this is also surely the wrong question on which to focus. The current discipline of the Church is directly a result of the unhealthy culture that underpins it, and it is not at all clear that refusing to abide by rules that spring out of this culture is entirely opposed to the role of faithful clergy.

One other specific situation is worth raising at this stage. Some have called for all clergy to be forced into civil partnerships if they are living with a partner, or – if and when the prohibition on civil marriage is permitted – to enforce this as the way of life for LGBTQI couples. This is to fundamentally misunderstand and misjudge the current societal and familial pressures and prejudices that many LGBTQI people continue to face, and is another example of the crass ecclesial arrogance that so often accompanies this debate, as if the only thing LGBTQI people are waiting for is the blessing of the Church. Huge barriers remain in place for LGBTQI people societally, both in the UK and abroad, and it is a fantasy to suggest that their lives are considered with anything like equality by society at large. The sad reality is that the Church could be an agent of their liberation in wider society but refuses to be so – but if and when the Church changes its position on this, then it would be double violence to imagine LGBTQI people have anything like a secure place in society and can be immediately treated as though they face no discrimination. It is of fundamental importance that the Church recognises this fundamental power imbalance, both within and without its walls. Openness is the goal, but the Church cannot drop its pastoral sensitivity in a misguided drive towards its singular vision of what this openness looks like. There will be situations when marriage or civil partnership is not appropriate because of this discrimination outside the Church, and it is for the Church to recognise this and respond appropriately. LGBTQI people remain oppressed, and it is simply absurd to think otherwise.

It is important here to recognise that the opening up of marriage to LGBTQI people is not a panacea and nor is the blessing of same-sex partnerships. The culture of homophobia and oppression is not going to be blown away overnight, but, nonetheless, a church that takes active steps to bless and openly celebrate LGBTQI people is taking a first step on that journey in cultural change. For the lonely gay child facing opposition from family and church alike, the simple act of seeing 'people like them' being held up as examples and rejoiced with is a very powerful thing. It is shameful that they might now see this in wider society, and yet the gates of the Church remain slammed shut. Blessings, then, are not the answer – but they are most definitely a part of it.

The position of the Church as it currently stands is one that attempts to make people grateful for the crumbs thrown to them. These might be situations in which blessings are undertaken in a hush-hush way, or where a civil partnership is tolerated but never celebrated. The Church must move beyond this to a place where the good that is happening is recognised and celebrated, and where LGBTQI people are not treated as second-class citizens whose lives are merely stomached rather than seen as places of great joy and creativity – lives which embody faith, hope and love. It is not the lives of LGBTQI people that must change in terms of substance – it would, rather, be a change in the ability and willingness of the Church to recognise what is already happening within them. LGBTQI people are invited guests at the table – and it is Christ, not the Church, who is the host. Threats and political demands appear wildly at odds with the gentle Christ that the Church is called to follow:

'Come to me, all you that are weary and are carrying heavy burdens, and I will give you rest. Take my yoke upon you, and learn from me; for I am gentle and humble in heart, and you will find rest for your souls. For my yoke is easy, and my burden is light.'

(Matthew 11:28-30)

One problem that we face when we look at the history of the Church is how to reconcile its beautiful place in the history of salvation with the appalling attitudes and acts perpetrated in its name. LGBTQI people are just the most recent in a long litany of people trampled over and scapegoated by the Church. Discussions about the infallible nature of the Church and its mission could (and do) generate many books and articles, but for our purposes the clear fact of the Church corporate having been in error in the past simply points to the need for a holy humility when it speaks. It is God who is the objective, divine truth, and the Church is humankind's organ for trying to delve ever deeper into God's revelation through scripture, tradition, and reason. Even a brisk traipse through the Church's history is enough to make us very cautious, and only a fool would claim to be able to read the mind of God, however illustrious their instruction or popular their reading of scripture.

This holy humility reminds us that there is a significant place for nuance and indeed doubt in the life of the Church. As we know from the lives of the saints, people are infrequently (indeed, never) all good or all bad, and what appears to be a predominantly virtuous life in one generation may be seen as quite the opposite in a later one – both within the Church and outside of it. Humility allows us to foster a sense of openness with our fellow Christians, and to recognise the importance of respecting those with whom we disagree, and not only on our terms. As we mentioned at the start of this book, human beings love certainty, yet the religious life – and the life of the Church – is one that points towards contingency, even encouraging us to learn to love the grey area where certainty and truth belongs to God alone. The words 'in my opinion' or 'I believe' are essential to any serious theological discussion, as is our willingness for correction and for our ideas to be properly challenged and refined. Our arguments are not always self-evident, and we must carefully listen to those with whom we debate and disagree if we are to truly live out our lives as faithful followers of the one who calls us.

Talk of humility, contingency and listening necessitate a brief discussion of a thorny issue that has not yet been raised. Throughout this book we have spoken extensively of relational sexuality, and it is important as we come towards our conclusion to refer to the obvious point that, for many – particularly those outside the household of faith but also those within – not all sexual behaviour is described or experienced in the context of a long-term, stable relationship, and, indeed, the idea that it must be is roundly rejected. This is without doubt the topic for another book; however, it is worth recognising this point and asking whether we can quite so easily roundly reject it.

We have seen throughout this book that sexuality is intimately bound up with the sense of self of an individual, and that the out-workings of relationality will often involve a sexual element (and it is demonstrably the case that this occurs even where the activity is not primarily or even consciously sexual in nature). We have already shown the fallacy of the position that states that sexual behaviour is discrete and separable from relational human expression; psychological theory suggests that the picture may be more complex still, with overtly sexual behaviours being part of a continuum that affects, most, if not all, human relationality. Through these pages we have focused on the most common Christian understanding of that out-working – sexual behaviour in the context of stable monogamy.

However, we must be alert to the principles that flow through this book and recognise that any argument that is made in favour of marriage as a specific manifestation of relational sexuality must constantly engage and dialogue with human experience and take seriously claims of healthy sexuality outside of these confines. Indeed, blessing relationships which are not defined as marriages (for example Civil Partnerships) requires us to think very carefully about what we are actually blessing and what this tells us about the defects – or otherwise – in our theology. If we bless them but still forbid sexual activity within them, then we appear to have learnt nothing at all about relational sexuality. It may be that this is a place where the grey area and contingency of theological development is quite apt – but this will require bishops to explicitly commend this to their clergy, and require a recognition that life is not as simple as a checklist. It is arguably more of a change to bless sexually active civil partnerships than it is to simply bring same-sex couples into the fold of marriage. Whatever the Church does decide, however, needs to hold any grey area together with absolute integrity. It must be an intentional grey area, rather than a hidden one – one that is named and not disguised. If clergy (and others) are legitimately expressing relational sexuality within blessed unions that the Church will not call marriage, then we must say so and affirm it.

It is well beyond the scope of this book to engage with these questions in detail, but not to highlight them would be disingenuous and against the entire flow of the argument in this chapter and more widely. The Christian answer to 'can sex ever be right outside of marriage?' has classically been an unqualified 'no', although it is not at all clear that theory and practice have coincided in any serious manner. It is, indeed, for this reason that so much has been made of the importance of marriage in homosexual relationships – marriage is the place for sexual expression, and therefore for homosexual sexual expression to ever be right, the only place for this must be marriage. We must make it abundantly clear that the question of sex outside of marriage is not a question that relates solely to LGBTQI people, although it is certainly true that the basic refusal of the Church to grant them any legitimacy or recognise their human dignity has meant that this community has perhaps more intentionally considered this question than those for whom marriage provides a convenient cover.

Yet to discard this question out of hand without showing our working is also increasingly unsustainable as a position for the Church to hold. The immediate response to any argument that posits 'the right place for sex is within marriage' is to ask the simple question: why? The Church can no longer simply repeat platitudes or make sweeping references to scripture, most particularly given all we have discussed in this book. It is perhaps one of the gifts of LGBTQI people to the Church that the Church needs to refocus its mind on these questions and develop a theology of sex and marriage that does not simply make constant reference to 'genital acts' between two people of the same sex.

Given the Church of England's acceptance of contraception and the change in our thinking on fornication and the joy of sex (as in the last chapter),[7] it is critical that the Church thinks more deeply about these questions. Whether sex must always be relational – and whether that relationality, if it is required, must take a particular form – is a key question for contemporary culture, yet it is a question that the Church has consistently failed to answer in any serious or convincing manner. Our focus on the need for 'marriage' may prove conclusive to some, but we need to urgently hold our arguments from scripture and tradition up against reason and experience if we are to provide anything that is remotely convincing in the apologetic realm.

It is for this reason that we must engage maturely with the scientific and sociological literature about forms of relationality and sexuality beyond those with which the Church has usually concerned itself. The Church's understanding and teaching in this area is extremely limited – embarrassingly so – because of its continued squeamishness about sex more generally and theological opposition to sex outside of marriage. However, to ignore something does not mean

---

[7] Readers may be interested in Harries, R., 'The Anglican acceptance of contraception', *Transformation: An International Journal of Holistic Mission Studies* (1996) 13 (3):2-4.

that it is not happening, and studies in the secular literature may well have a lot of say to the Church – whether that is in supporting its current doctrine or encouraging an openness to revisit what is held to be essential from tradition, and fundamental to scriptural interpretation, in the light of new human insights. If the Church is to offer teaching on sexuality and relationships, it must seek to genuinely understand that of which it speaks – anything less is simply an abrogation of responsibility and an insult to the tradition of Christian theology.[8]

The Church also needs to make a serious commitment to discerning our understanding of what marriage actually is, and what we mean by it – for example, whether the ceremony fundamentally changes a relationship or whether it is rather the recognition of the state of being that in some way pre-exists. If the former, no sex before marriage is a simpler position to hold, albeit one that few people – Christians included – abide by. If the latter, then the position begins to look somewhat more tenuous. The point of raising this is not to attempt to pronounce definitively on it, but rather to demand that these questions are taken more seriously. It is quite simply unacceptable that the Church of England's thinking and position on marriage and sex appears to primarily focus on what LGBTQI people cannot do.

Finally in this chapter, we turn to the question of what inclusion and inclusivity means, in the context of all that has been said. It is likely that in the next few years, churches of many denominations will need to find ways to keep as many people as possible – with many different views on LGBTQI people and indeed other issues – within the fold. In the first instance, a truly inclusive community must be one that rejects any interpretation of scripture that demands absolute obedience, and that can only ever ultimately be one based

---

[8] The reader's attention is once again drawn to Thatcher, A. (ed.), *The Oxford Handbook of Theology, Sexuality, and Gender* for an exploration of these themes.

on the whim – however well informed – of humankind. This is fundamentally in opposition to the Bible's own self-identity, and any 'Christianities' that demand such loyalty are little more than cults, built on sand. Christianity – our seeking to discern the mind of God as revealed – is by nature contingent, grace-filled, openminded and openhearted, and a gift from God. It is never the property of any one individual, charismatic leader, or school of thought – it is the preserve of Christ Jesus. The universal church, through the guidance of the Holy Spirit, has access to the scriptures, to the tradition of its members, to reason and experience, and to the credal formulations. Beyond these creeds, there are no foundational articles of belief, and there is no test of orthodoxy. To base orthodoxy on the sex-lives of LGBTQI people is nothing short of blasphemy.

We have seen the importance of not just naming but addressing power imbalances above. Just as vital, however, is the need to recognise that an inclusive church is one in which oppressed groups are not pitted against each other – indeed, an inclusive church is one in which each such group acts as an ally to the others, and, indeed, seeks allyship from those in the dominant group. This is true Christian solidarity, and it is only by listening to and responding to the calls and cries of different downtrodden people that we can ever truly find both common ground and build up the body of Christ. It should not only be LGBTQI people who stand up for LGBTQI people; it should not only be black people who stand up for black people; the list is endless. To truly fight oppression is to fight all oppression, and it is inevitable that many of the situations highlighted in this book apply to other oppressed groups beyond LGBTQI Christians. We should be standing up for one another, and it is only then that we can claim to be inclusive. Our responsibility is to our common life, as well as our individual freedom. Liberation comes through liberating all, not only those like us. It is for this reason that intersectionality is so important.[9]

[9] Of interest may be Romero, M., *Introducing Intersectionality* (Hoboken: Wiley, 2017).

It is, thus, totally fallacious to argue that LGBTQI issues are not 'the priority' when faced with a host of other important issues – far too often, straight clergy talk about how they wish the Church could talk about the 'bigger issues' instead of 'obsessing about sexuality'. This kind of language is an insult and must stop – it is easy to ignore and downplay the oppression when you are not being oppressed. Pushing for change for LGBTQI people does not somehow mean that there is not also a focus on feeding the hungry, highlighting the plight of the poor or caring for the environment. Indeed, if we do not sort our own house out, then our moral stands on these issues will fall on deaf ears.

The wider world has learnt much about intersectionality in recent years – yet another reason that we would do well to listen to secular wisdom. Until we recognise that we need to be intersectional in our opposition to oppression, we will simply replace one system of oppression with another. True change will come about when the rules of engagement change – when we become a truly Eucharistic community. If we ignore the oppression of our fellow Christians, then we are not working for true liberation but rather for a shifting of the balance, and the shouldering of oppression by others. Our fellow subjugated siblings are a corrective and remind us of the key place of reconciliation in the heart of the Church. We are all part of a system of structural oppression – this is not something over which to self-flagellate, but it is something about which to take action. 'I'm all right, Jack' is not the way of the Kingdom of God.

That the Church continues to oppress and participate in wider societal oppression is a scandal, yet the lives of those who bear that yoke are a gift to the Church. Faithful Christians continue to worship God and work for the Kingdom despite everything the Church throws at them. This very faithfulness holds the key to the releasing of the Church's bondage, and it is to this that we turn in our final chapter.

13

THE EXTRAORDINARY GIFT

We started this book by stating the obvious: the history of the Church and LGBTQI people is not a happy one. Throughout these pages we have seen plenty of examples that suggest that the present Church's relationship with LGBTQI people is not much better either. We have seen signs and symptoms of quite severe illness, yet the treatment – and dare I say even the cure – is not beyond our grasp. This will be a holistic treatment, for sure – one that takes into account the entire body of Christ – each of its members, the way each react, relate, and respond to the other, and the way it defines itself. This is certainly no small task, yet it is a vital one if we are not to enter intensive care.

Throughout this book, too, we have seen what an enormous gift LGBTQI people and their experience are to the life of the body of Christ. Oppression rarely occurs in a vacuum – what we have seen says much about the whole functioning of the Church and its culture. The structural oppression of LGBTQI people is, in many ways, just one facet of a wider sickness, a sickness that threatens to overwhelm us if it is not both recognised and fought against. The Church doesn't need to be like this – indeed, it surely cannot survive much longer if the rot continues to spread. This book has sketched out a way forward, and agree or disagree with this way forward, we must at least recognise that the problem is real.

LGBTQI people in this book have been met as individuals

– as integrated children of God – and not 'issues', 'problems' or 'discussion topics'. This is essential as we move forward and, unless and until the rest of the Church can see LGBTQI people as guests at the table of the Lord – guests as equally favoured, loved and cherished as anyone else at that table – then we blaspheme and mar the face of God. These are strong claims, but they are grafted in the words of scripture and in the entire history of Christian thought and practice. It is remarkable that, despite everything, still we find bombastic straight people attempting to lord it over the lives of LGBTQI faithful Christians. Introspection, self-doubt, humility – all these are holy virtues – and all these are lacking from far too many powerful voices in God's church.

So the Church must find some way to do theology about sexuality alongside and with LGBTQI people, who we treat as equals and as full members of the Church, and not lesser or problematic. The body of Christ is diminished when we try to take the place of the host instead of Christ Himself; it is hopelessly incomplete when LGBTQI people dare not even come through the door. The can-kicking and the argument that 'there are more important things to worry about' are both damaging to real LGBTQI lives, and to the life of the Church more widely. It is time to take some action, and to start talking about belonging as well as inclusion. LGBTQI people are not some external group that need to be made to feel 'included' in the Church – they are already children of God, and it is the responsibility of the Church to recognise them as that rather than create its own list of commandments to allow them entry. LGBTQI people are not sick, they are not intrinsically disordered, they are not any more mired in sin than others are – they are God's beloved children. It is God's table, and God's Church – and it is time we remembered this.

What is truly remarkable, when we think about LGBTQI people and the Church, is how faithful so many remain in the face of discrimination and hatred. LGBTQI people continue to serve the Church in all its ministries, and continue to offer themselves patiently and sacrificially in debates about their very identity. LGBTQI people continue to speak truth and lose any chance of preferment – they continue to raise issues of power and oppression, even when it makes others feel deeply uncomfortable. As we have seen, their experience in the Church is a gift to it. It can only be of God that they continue, steadfastly and faithfully, to bear witness to the love of Christ and hold a mirror up to the sickness still found in the Church. It is quite wrong to mistake their challenge to the Church as an attempt to bring it down. On the contrary, so many LGBTQI people still love the Church – if they didn't then they would walk away.

The Church, though, including the Church of England, needs to take stock of what it has done to its LGBTQI members – and more widely, to LGBTQI people who it has scared away from hearing the Good News. It has frequently denied their baptismal vocation as Christians, it has thrown vague notions of 'unity' at them and demanded silence from those who are appointed as bishops, it has thrown political documents dressed up as theology at them, it has been willing to throw them under the bus in the name of the greater good. They have even been told that their human dignity will have to await a mythical council of the universal church – whilst a host of other issues can apparently be decided closer to home. They are expendable. 'You do not understand that it is better for you to have one man die for the people than to have the whole nation destroyed' (John 11:50) has been employed again and again at the expense of LGBTQI people, who have been sacrificed in the name of the Church – not a good look for Caiaphas the High Priest, and not a good look for the twenty-first century Church. Yet LGBTQI people still show up. There's your miracle.

The Church needs to radically return to the sources and breathe in the signs of the times. It is time for the cries of sin and repentance to turn away from LGBTQI people and towards the Church. The Church has gotten this wrong for too long, and it is time for it to turn back towards the Lord, the scriptures, the tradition, experience, and reason, and ask for forgiveness. It is only through naming the sin and through true repentance that reconciliation can come.

LGBTQI people should be commended for their witness to a life of love, lived in the grace and power of God. Their lives continue to bring light to a messy, divided institution that reflects something of the glory of its institutor, Christ Jesus. Their lives challenge cultural and theological norms and point to the need for the Church to step outside its comfort zone and embrace wider learning and human knowledge. They help the Church 'get over itself' in a way that is not only beneficial but essential. Theology locked in a cave says much about the cave, but little about the world outside. It is unsustainable for us to continue in that way.

Yet the Church has spent so long judging the lives and loves of LGBTQI people that it fails to recognise that it itself might be part of the problem. Scare tactics, half-truths and outright lies continue to define the way that LGBTQI lives – and their sex lives in particular – are discussed. LGBTQI people's sex lives continue to be described in gratuitously offensive and unevidenced ways,[1] as though they are an especially promiscuous group of people engaging in disgusting, depraved and disease-laden sexual practices. We have already discussed the inadequacy of a theology of disgust. Beneath the surface, the prejudice and hatred of the AIDS epidemic continues to bubble – indeed, it is outrageous that only one cathedral in the UK (Southwark) has a memorial to the victims of that terrible epidemic. Yet whilst Christians continue to look down their noses at the sexual lives of LGBTQI people, the reality is that the Church has entirely failed to offer any kind of positive view of sexuality to LGBTQI people, preferring instead to declare the whole thing as sinful and disgusting.

[1] A particularly heinous example of this is the selective and ultimately misleading use of scientific and sociological literature mixed with what is little more than thinly veiled prejudice in the shockingly disingenuous final chapter (The Hermeneutical Relevance of the Biblical Witness) of Robert Gagnon's *The Bible and Homosexual Practice* (2001).

It is here that we must discuss the somewhat thorny issue of living with difference in the Church. Those advocating for a change in attitude and behaviour towards LGBTQI people must be wary of making demands of those who disagree with them which end up looking remarkably like those they have spent their time opposing. The Church, if it is to be a place of openness, cannot simply stop theological conversation from happening. However, there are important things to remember when thinking through the relationship between different theologies. In the first instance, it is certainly the case that some theologies offer a demonstrably narrower vision of human life than others, and some promote forms of living that are – if taken to their natural conclusion – psychologically and culturally damaging. It is hard to look a gay teenager, who attends a church that calls them intrinsically disordered, in the eye and say there must be room for all theologies in the Church. Yet likewise, the entire thrust of this book has been one that calls for debate, contingency, and learning.

There are various ways through what initially appears to be a very significant point of tension. In the first instance, we must demand more rigorous thought be given to the presentation of and the development of our theological viewpoints, and in the way that we present them in dialogue. If that gay teenager were to be told – 'this is our view, and we hold it strongly, but there are others, and here is someone who could tell you about it' – then we find ourselves in a fundamentally different position. This is challenging, of course, for those who think they are right, but the Anglican way is one of dialogue and holy humility. We do not win people for Christ by pretending there are no other arguments, rubbishing others, or steamrolling people. If our arguments are to hold weight, then they must be tried and tested in conversation and debate, and in the light of their fruits as well. This is what radical openness looks like, and if we are to live together with disagreements in this matter, then we need to be open and honest in all our doings. We may be wrong – all of us.

This is also a healthier model for engaging with the

wider world. Many Christians seem disappointed and even confused that more people do not come to Christ in the contemporary age. One possible reason for this is that we have simply not shown that the way of Christ is more life-giving than any other. In our debates with the wider world, we must be honest, open, respectful and engage with the actual arguments presented, rather than creating our own straw men. Yet whilst our arguments are important, ultimately people want to see the life of Christ in our lives as well as in our preaching. It is for this reason that mission is not simply evangelism, and if we are not convincing people with our lives then shouting louder is not going to help (and nor is any amount of imported pop culture in our worship). If our lives are not attractive, we need to ask why – and not simply bemoan contemporary culture.

The purpose of this book is to fire the starting gun on these conversations and call us to a more mature engagement with the world, rather than provide definitive answers. In a sense, however, any conversations on these issues are going to remain, by nature, contingent. Yet, together with 'sorry', contingency does appear to be the hardest word for some people vehemently opposed to LGBTQI liberation. As we have discussed, it is simply untrue and un-biblical to argue that there is one, definitive, unshakeable, and clear interpretation of scripture, and similarly it is in the eye of the interpreter, and dependent on their hermeneutic, what the Bible has to say about same-sex relationships. Yet this is very different to saying that the Bible is not true. Each time we go to the Bible to find answers to our questions, we make choices – unconscious or otherwise – about where to look, what to consider relevant to the question at hand (the ancient debate about the meaning and place of the Song of Songs is a good example)[2], and how the text should

---

[2] The history of this marvellous yet somewhat mystifying book is well told in Pardes, I., *The Song of Songs: A Biography* (Princeton: Princeton University Press, 2019).

be read. A denial of this is simply self-deception. The whole process is one of discernment, and to try to claim even a remote element of objectivity is demonstrably untrue.

It is self-evident that many parts of scripture appear contradictory and may appear to point in different directions. This is not a new insight – indeed, the Church Fathers grappled with this precise issue, and yet resolved it by recognising their inability to read the mind of God.

> *Since I am entirely convinced that no Scripture contradicts another, I shall admit that I do not understand what is recorded, and shall strive to persuade those who imagine that the Scriptures are contradictory, to be rather of the same opinion of myself. (Justin – Dialogue, 65)*
>
> *We should leave things [of an unknowable] nature to God who creates us, being most assured that the Scriptures are indeed perfect, since they were spoken by the Word of God and His Spirit.(Irenaeus – Against Heresies, 2.38.2)*

Yet the fathers also recognised that the scriptures are 'true utterances of the Holy Spirit' (Clement of Rome), and the cornerstone of our faith:

> *For if I say something that unquestionably contradicts Sacred Scripture, I am certain that it is false; and I do not want to hold that view if I know it [to be false].(Anselm – Cur Deus Homo)*

That there are a variety of interpretations and thus possible understandings is not, then, the same as stating that the Bible is untrue. Likewise, it is not the same as saying that God has changed His mind. However, it is a recognition that the Bible is of God and from God, and God owes us the clarity we demand no more than he owes us anything else. God is Truth, and Christ is the Word of God – this truth has been revealed in the scriptures and continues to be revealed in the work of the Holy Spirit throughout the ages. This revelation must be – by nature – concordant – and it is for this reason that we must be constantly alert to the work of the Spirit and willing to wrestle with scripture, placing it into dialogue with our knowledge and understanding of the world. The Church has changed its mind through history on many issues, but it is not God who was mistaken – it was the Church. The continual discernment of the will of God is the fruit of the Spirit, and we fundamentally devalue the Bible if we see it as anything other than living, relevant and constantly being revealed ever more and more. The deposit of faith is one that allows us to continually contemplate the mind of God, and to exclude human knowledge and understanding from this deposit is to reject a tool that God has given us.

It is for this reason that an appeal to take experience, discovery and reason seriously is anything but revisionism. We must ask ourselves whether theology can really afford to ignore the insights of science and human experience any longer when these very insights are the gift of God Himself. Such a theology is not only deficient but fundamentally untheological, and we need to grapple with all that God gives rather than pick and choose. Scripture remains the prime authority, but to come to scripture without all the tools we have in our toolkit seems a fundamentally bizarre way to think about God. All interpretations of scripture are coloured by our humanity – it is surely essential for us to come fully prepared and with our eyes open to the reality of the world.

We ultimately find ourselves at a time when the Church must make a choice – do we retreat into history books and a facile biblicism or do we meet the world head on, as a church that takes the whole of creation, revelation, and salvation seriously? Do we hold to the three-legged stool, or do we attempt to determine the meaning of scripture without reference to reason? What, ultimately, do we call 'orthodox' – is it the peripherals or is it the core of the Gospel message?

It is the argument of this book that we must regain our

prophetic voice. LGBTQI people are prophets to the Church, and to listen to them means being willing to take a prophetic stand as the Church corporate. The church cannot go on as it has been – it is unsustainable and eventually the wheels will come off. 'When the Spirit of truth comes, he will guide you into all the truth' (John 16:13) – the question is whether we will be willing to listen.

God has blessed LGBTQI people and continues to lead them into the promised land – as honoured guests at the table of the Lord. Christ speaks to His church and says – follow me. The time is ripe, and God is calling us to leave aside our fear and our power, and taste and see how good He is. He is calling His church home, and He is proclaiming liberty to the captives. He waits to welcome us to his sacred heart: queer, faithful, Christian, beloved.

> Is not this the fast that I choose:
> to loose the bonds of injustice,
> to undo the thongs of the yoke,
> to let the oppressed go free,
> and to break every yoke?
>
> (Isaiah 58:6)

RECOMMENDED BIBLIOGRAPHY

1. Ainsworth, C., 'Sex redefined', *Nature* (2015) 518:288-291
2. Avis, P., *In Search of Authority* (London: Bloomsbury Academic, 2014)
3. Balthazart, J., *The Biology of Homosexuality* (Oxford: Oxford University Press, 2011)
4. Barmash, P. (ed.), *The Oxford Handbook of Biblical Law* (Oxford: OUP, 2019)
5. Barton, J., *A History of the Bible* (London: Penguin, 2019)
6. Beeley, C.A., 'Christ and Human Flourishing in Patristic Theology', *Pro Ecclesia: A Journal of Catholic and Evangelical Theology* (2016) 25 (2): 126-153
7. *Book of Common Prayer (1662)* (Cambridge: Cambridge University Press, 2004)
8. Brouwer, S., Gifford, P., Rose, S. D., *Exporting the American Gospel* (Abingdon: Taylor & Francis, 2013)
9. Brown, T., ed., *Other Voices, Other Worlds: Global Church Speaks out on Homosexuality* (London: Darton, Longman and Todd, 2006)
10. Burke, P., ed., *Contemporary Social Psychological Theories* (Stanford: Stanford University Press, 2006)
11. Chapman, M., *Anglican Theology* (London: Bloomsbury Publishing, 2012)
12. Chitando, E., and van Klinken, A. (eds.), *Christianity and Controversies over Homosexuality in Contemporary Africa* (Oxford: Routledge, 2016)
13. Davey, G. C., *Psychology* (London: Wiley, 2018)
14. Decety, J., and Ickes, W., eds., *The Social Neuroscience of Empathy* (Boston: MIT, 2009)
15. Eskridge Jr, W. N., and Spedale, D. R., *Gay Marriage: For Better or for Worse?* (Oxford: Oxford University Press, 2006)
16. Estes, J., *Anglican Manifesto* (Eugene: Wipf and Stock, 2014)
17. Ford, M., *God, Gender, Sex and Marriage* (London: Jessica Kingsley, 2018)
18. Ganna, A., et al., 'Large-scale GWAS reveals insights into the genetic architecture of same-sex sexual behavior', *Science* (2019) 365 (6456)
19. Girard, R., *The Scapegoat* (Washington DC: Johns Hopkins University Press, 1989)
20. Greenough, C., *Queer Theologies: The Basics* (London: Routledge, 2019)
21. Haldeman, D. C., ed., *The Case Against Conversion 'Therapy': Evidence, Ethics, and Alternatives* (Washington DC: APA, 2021)
22. Harries, R., 'The Anglican acceptance of contraception', *Transformation: An International Journal of Holistic Mission Studies* (1996) 13 (3):2-4
23. Hentschel, U., et al, eds., *The Concept of Defence Mechanisms in Contemporary Psychology* (New York: Springer, 1993)
24. Herbert, C., *Towards a Theology of Same-Sex Marriage* (London: Jessica Kingsley, 2020)

25. Hoad, N., et al, eds., *Sex and Politics in South Africa* (Cape Town: Double Storey, 2005)

26. Issenberg, S., *The Engagement* (New York: Knopf Doubleday, 2021)

27. Keen, K., *Scripture, Ethics, and the Possibility of Same-Sex Relationships* (Grand Rapids: Eerdmans, 2018)

28. Lytle M. C., et al, 'Association of Religiosity with Sexual Minority Suicide Ideation and Attempt', *American Journal of Preventative Medicine* (2018) 54 (5) pp. 644-651

29. MacCulloch, D., *A History of Christianity: The First Three Thousand Years* (Oxford: OUP, 2010)

30. Maltby, J., *Prayer Book and People in Elizabethan and Early Stuart England* (Cambridge: CUP, 1998)

31. Martin, J., *Building a Bridge* (San Francisco: HarperOne, 2018)

32. Massmann, A., and Fox, K. R., *Modifying Our Genes: Theology, Science and 'Playing God'* (London: SCM Press, 2021)

33. Morvan, C., and O'Connor, A., *An Analysis of Leon Festinger's A Theory of Cognitive Dissonance* (London: Macat, 2017)

34. Nussbaum, M. C., *From Disgust to Humanity: Sexual Orientation and Constitutional Law* (Oxford: Oxford University Press, 2010)

35. O'Collins, G., *The Second Vatican Council: Message and Meaning* (Collegeville: Liturgical Press, 2014)

36. Pardes, I., *The Song of Songs: A Biography* (Princeton: Princeton University Press, 2019)

37. Romero, M., *Introducing Intersectionality* (Hoboken: Wiley, 2017)

38. Selby, P., *BeLonging: Challenge to a Tribal Church* (London: SPCK, 1991)

39. Sigurdson, O., *Heavenly Bodies: Incarnation, the Gaze, and Embodiment in Christian Theology* (Grand Rapids: Eerdmans, 2016)

40. Singer, J., ed., *Repression and Dissociation* (Chicago: University of Chicago Press, 1995)

41. Sommer, V., and Vasey, P. L. (eds.), *Behaviour in Animals: An Evolutionary Perspective* (Cambridge: Cambridge University Press, 2006)

42. Thatcher, A. (ed.), *The Oxford Handbook of Theology, Sexuality, and Gender* (Oxford: Oxford University Press, 2015)

43. Todd, M., *Straight Jacket* (London: Penguin, 2018)

44. Volf, M., *Exclusion and Embrace* (Nashville: Abingdon, 1996)

45. Warner, M., 'Therefore a Man Leaves His Father and His Mother and Clings to His Wife': Marriage and Intermarriage in Genesis 2:24 *JBL* (2017) 136 (2): 269-288

46. Wilson, G., and Rahman, Q., *Born Gay: the Psychobiology of Sex Orientation* (London: Peter Owen, 2008)

47. Yrigoyen Jr, C. (ed.), *T & T Clark Companion to Methodism* (London: Bloomsbury T & T Clark, 2014)